Remembering Walter Carrington

Remembering Walter Carrington

Keystone of the Alexander Technique

Compiled and edited by
Elizabeth Langford

Alexandertechniek Centrum vzw
Leuven
2006

Published by
Alexandertechniek Centrum vzw
Leopold Beosierlaan 57
B-3010 Leuven (Kessel-Lo)
Belgium
Tel./fax +32 1625 1289
Design and layout by Monique Vanormelingen
Printed by Acco Leuven

Cover photo: Walter on Badger © Stephen Parker
Cover photos of Walter's hands © Noel Kingsley
Back cover: photo of Lansdowne Road garden © Susan Cohen

Orders: info@alexandertechniquecentre.be
Web-site: http://www.alexandertechniquecentre.be

D/2006/8501/4
ISBN 90-808491-2-X

Table of Contents

Introduction

G.K. Chesterton wrote concerning the arch in Gothic architecture:
"The principle asserts that by combining separate stones of a particular shape in a particular way, we can ensure that their very tendency to fall shall prevent them from falling".

That sentence delighted Walter. It suggests an analogy with the natural tendency of the human head to fall freely with its own weight, according to the natural limits of the atlanto-occipital joint - an important factor in maintaining our physical balance. It further suggests that respect for the nature of individual freedom should assist our mental and moral balance. In building a Gothic cathedral, each stone had its own individual shape and nature; its own tendencies were to be respected. Nobody understood better than Walter that the same is true of Alexander teachers. He accepted that it must be so.

Perhaps acceptance was not always as easy as he made it look. "Well, Betty", he said to me once, "if you do potty work, you meet potty people." It was his light-hearted way of reminding me that each person brings personal ways of understanding that can serve the Technique and help others. Walter's keynote speech at the 2004 International Congress emphasized the individual nature of our work. People capable of devoting themselves to something as far ahead of its time as the Alexander Technique are by nature highly individual.

They must each be given the opportunity to learn in a way that suits them. Only thus can they grow into the degree of personal responsibility that is implied in the Technique itself. Walter's teaching style was coloured by his awareness of that fact. Hence his former students have been able to write, "You knew he was working to help you, not to impress you" and "Most teachers try to teach you; Walter gave you room to learn". Walter trusted our capacity to go on thinking - each at our own pace. He thought it unwise to sacrifice individual thinking and learning on the altar of conformity to "modern" society. Latterly, he was sad to note such tendencies making an appearance even among Alexander teachers.

Walter, while remaining completely himself, always found a way to relate to anyone he was talking to: he had such a remarkable ability to make associations and connections. Christopher, his eldest son, has spoken of his father's many interests. Daniel Pevsner has mentioned how much horse-riding contributed to Walter's teaching skills - I know the truth of that, from several recent lessons. My impression is that everything that held any interest for Walter was grist to his mill, in the sense that any of his many interests, when exposed to the light of his continuous awareness of the Alexander Technique, could suggest something valuable for his teaching. Thus, a schoolboy memory of choir singing could be used in good voice production - alongside his memories of F.M. Alexander quoting Shakespeare, and probably associated with stored up memories of the varied vocal delivery of those who preached the sermons he had heard in his youth. Thus, while watching a video of David Oistrakh, Walter, harking back to a conversation long ago, asked me to confirm his observation of how the great violinist was supporting his violin. Walter's letters testify to his wide reading: animal behaviour, mathematics, neuroscience, palaeontology, philosophy

– you name it. Whatever it was, if it had a bearing on the Alexander Technique, Walter wanted to know more about it, and was ready to share the knowledge if he saw your interest aroused. So a discussion of head posture could produce from his files a paper on pterosaurs – or I once saw him demonstrate how a ballerina achieves a pirouette!

Alexander teachers all over the world were glad that *The Times* had honoured Walter with an obituary running to four full columns. We were glad, too, when Christine Ackers let us see her own spontaneous reaction, more personal than *The Times* could ever be. As soon as I read it, I wrote to her saying, "I'm sure you were there when ...". She replied, "All this must be collected – but how?"

That was the start of this book, which could have continued to grow indefinitely. People who never met Walter have written because they have read his books, or because they have learnt the Technique from someone who studied with him. I am deeply grateful to Dilys Carrington and her family for entrusting to me the editing of these recollections. I count myself particularly fortunate in that reading other people's memories has sparked off so many of my own. My sincere thanks to all who have contributed, and to Monique Vanormelingen for undertaking the endless chores associated with layout and printing.

The dictionary tells us that a keystone, literally, is the central stone at the summit of an arch locking the whole together. Figuratively, it is the central principle of a system, policy, etc. on which all the rest depends. It seems natural to think of Walter in those terms. That is partly what makes it so hard to reconcile oneself to his passing. Things he explained, jokes he made, stories he told, moments significant to us individually, help us to remember what we learnt from him. Of course we share a natural impulse to offer to his memory this tribute of our love and respect. Beyond that, we find it important to offer, to those who did not have the good fortune to know him, our limited sketches of a man who was the personification of the Alexander Technique.

Elizabeth Langford
April 2006

Christine Ackers

No, we cannot feel wholly sad. If he taught us anything, it was the usefulness of putting a positive spin on things. Of course he was an exceptional exponent of F.M. Alexander's work. His marvellously spread hands, gentle as a baby's, packing the punch of a boxer's, were like none others in their capacity to blast away the normal collation of base desires and trivial concerns constituting one's mood. Warmth and laughter would course through you, enlarging your narrow internal world as your back lengthened and widened with fresh prospects. But it was his extraordinary tolerance of the human condition that pitched him into a more saintly realm. "Hallo, my dear, how simply lovely to see you!" became a sort of catch-cry experience as we were drenched over and over in the unflagging generosity and sincerity of his welcome. Good co-ordination and a singular lack of personality disorder seemed to have combined in this man to produce a deeply calming presence.

Walter was born in 1915, during the First World War - the one that was supposed to end them all - only to spend the first years of his manhood flying around Europe throughout the Second. Whether by nature or conscious decision, he grew to become everybody's friend. He is the one from amongst our golden oldies who, when asked on a video what he thought about the state of the Alexander Technique today, so memorably replied that he felt our differences were fewer than our common aims. Since our shared objective is to teach the Alexander Technique, the comment was irrefutable, leaving us with nothing further to do but get on with it! We bickering normals had been subtly disarmed.

At times, people wanted him to take more of a stand against, for instance, the depredations of the business-speak mentality upon the nobility of F.M. Alexander's contribution to human lore. Yet somehow he managed to endorse each individual's efforts to protect the work from debasement. It was just that he wouldn't join in the fray and call the others a bunch of shits. I suppose he'd seen enough of that during the first half of the twentieth century over parts of Germany, Italy and eastern Europe.

Was it as an alternative to that mayhem, perhaps, that he seized the means in Alexander's Indirect Method of developing a quite remarkable gift for diplomacy? Back in the 1960's, on a grey morning, while he worked on me, I was watching a fellow-student taking someone's head on the table. Her wrists were fixed, her eyes stared as she strained to "think up", while her own head was yanked firmly back and down by her tight front. In exasperation at her pathetic performance, my feelings surely compounded by the question as to whether I'd do any better myself, I let off a bit of steam in a general sort of way. "People," I spluttered, "are so bad at this!" I did not expect an answer exactly. But as usual, Wally was there for me; and after pondering and noting what I saw, he responded with, "Yes, my dear, you're quite right," – gently, kindly, acknowledging my perception. Then – thereby so skilfully obviating any negation of the other person's struggle, while simultaneously assuaging my beginner's frustration – he added, "But they are getting better".

For this man, the humanitarian consideration seemed always to take priority over the business of being right. When his own patience was tried, he'd work on a solution to the problem rather than use the opportunity to exercise a pompous authority. In those early days, he would start the session with a half-hour talk about the work, during which students would arrive, one at a time, punctuating each sentence of his chat or his reading with a shriek of the doorbell. This was irritating, and we who'd arrived on time would sit there fuelling our righteous annoyance with aggressive fantasies. But, perhaps to our disappointment, Walter simply moved the talk time half an hour forward, with the request that those who came even later should wait until after the session in a room downstairs.

When that didn't solve the problem - naturally, nobody wanted to sit alone missing the precious words, so each would creep into the room hoping not to be noticed in spite of having rung the doorbell anyway - perhaps he decided that the problem might as well be ignored. While our heads turned to glare at each entrant, he would calmly continue reading and talking, showing us how to not react. That's what he did mostly. He showed us. Years later when I told him how frustrated I was with one of my own trainees who didn't seem to be taking on board what I'd been battling to impart, he so gracefully lifted me off my hook with, "Well, my dear, one can only show them".

He stuck with what was relevant and therefore dealt with the important things. I received an early lesson in common sense from him when my first pupil asked me for coffee. The young man was handsome, I was excited, so the scary issue of "professional behaviour" loomed. I asked Walter whether I'd disgrace the Alexander establishment by going out with a pupil. "No, my dear – I don't see why that would be so", he replied, pondering. Then came the master-stroke of perspective: "You will only bring disgrace on the Alexander establishment if you give bad Alexander lessons."

He was having a giggle, but also meant it when he told us we mustn't mind our mistakes. "Life would be no fun at all if we weren't wrong," he said. "It would be game, set and match without having had the fun of playing!"

And was our great teacher intentionally droll when he asked me whether I could throw any light on why an applicant had been turned away from another training school on account of his being homosexual: "Now, I wouldn't have thought that had an awful lot to do with it, would you my dear?"

So we are sad, and somehow also glad – of the richness of having bathed in this man's beaming aura for such a long span. Yes, my dears, we have lost a good one; but there will be other good ones powering along in the pipeline. We must just go on. Yes, my dear......

Mary Holland

It was my great good fortune to have known Walter all my life, and with so many memories it was difficult to choose what to write. So finally I decided that the best way to honour him is to let him speak with his own words. Here is a selection of some of his sayings, as best as I can remember them, which have stayed with me over the years as constant encouraging companions.

Possibly the earliest comes from a lesson when I was very young:
What we want is for you to take up your share of space in the world.

This imaginative expression of going up and lengthening and widening has been an inspiration to me and many of my pupils.

Once, a few years later, after my lesson, he said:
Take some time for a little quiet thinking on those lines.

(I don't remember now what those lines were, but I do remember feeling rather horrified at the prospect of having to think – which made me think!)

During my training he suggested that we should ask ourselves the question:
What happens when I do nothing?

The next task he recommended to us can take a lifetime:
What you have got to do is to observe your behaviour, and from what you have observed deduce your unconscious beliefs.

Sometimes a sentence from one of his talks would come floating into my consciousness many years later, just when it was needed. For example:
If at some point in the lesson you do not know what to do with your pupil – take yourself up more.

One day he announced during one of his talks:
There are basically three ways of teaching anybody anything.
We all mentally got out our notebooks and pencils to make sure of remembering these three ways – and then had to laugh when he continued:
The first is by example. The second is by example. And the third is – by example!

This was of course how he taught us, by example.

Also amusing was:
The more people are out of touch with their bodies, the more they want to impress each other with their intellectual achievements.

The last few times that I saw him, some sentences that Walter said seemed to have an extraordinarily intense psycho-physical effect on me. It was as if the sound and meaning of the words were working in the way his hands had done when he was giving me lessons – freeing me and bringing about change.

One was:
This work is about identifying the wrong and allowing the right.

And the other was:
Some people are frightened of coming into contact with the Unknown. There is no need to be:

IT IS BENEFICENT.

Michael D. Frederick

August 7, 2005

Dear Walter,

Your assistant from Lansdowne Road, John Brown, phoned saying you died peacefully in your bed this morning at Charing Cross Hospital. Something we all expected - at 90 one is allowed to die. Still, the sadness intrudes alongside the joy of knowing you. The last man standing is now gone. At least the remembrances of your long and productive life can now be written about - especially your masterful Alexander teaching skills and your wonderful sense of humor. You have always brought about a lightness of heart, a lightness so often forgotten by the "serious" teachers of today. For me though, it was your humanity that overrides all and still lives.

In those happy years, in the mid 1970's, when Lena and I and our very new son John Michael lived in your top flat at Lansdowne Road, I was a witness to your everyday life. I can picture you getting up early to ride your horse in those leather boots - on the weekends wearing an ink-stained printers bib at your Sheildrake Press (located in that little cubby hole behind where your car was parked) - and typing away in the office on a Sunday afternoon, keeping on top of your voluminous correspondence - for once not wearing your customary three-piece suit and tie! A man ordinary to the point of being extraordinary. A rare kind of extraordinary. The masterful simplicity of living in the present moment - a quality that today is so fashionable to talk about, but unfortunately few achieve it.

Anicius Manlius Severinus Boethius - what a name - was the last of the great Roman philosophers and the first of the scholastics of the Middle Ages. Fifteen hundred years ago, Boethius wrote this sentence: "O happy race of mortals, if your hearts are ruled as is the universe by love". Walter, your kind heart was truly ruled by love.

There you were in the peaks and valleys of my life. You were so supportive when Lena died and then a few years later when John Michael took his own life. I still carry with me the e-mail you and Dilys sent, "Above all Michael, remember you are not to blame - no one is to blame". This always gives me solace. Walter, you taught us that guilt in life is a wasted emotion and that teaching which creates fear is ethically and morally unacceptable.

The other night, I watched in your honor the classic British movie, *Goodbye Mr. Chips,* about the kindly public school headmaster. At one point Chips says, "We must have hierarchies in life - we must have points of reference!" In hearing this I realized the importance of you, Walter, as a true "point of reference" - like the North Star - belonging to no one, but to all. Consistently simple, giving the rest of us a focus as we walk through our overly complicated lives. You were incredibly supportive of us all as individuals - not only in our lives, but especially in our Alexander teaching. You believed in the power of the individual - you believed in us, and our ability to think on our own. Something Mr. Chips would agree with.

Goodbye Walter and thank you. The honor and pleasure of knowing you continues...

With love, Michael Frederick

Meredith Page

Two days before I heard that Walter had had a serious fall and was not expected to recover, he had sent me an e-mail with an attachment concerning the aboriginal instrument, the didgeridoo. I, complacently, did not reply immediately. To my regret, I missed my last chance to thank and talk with him.

Several years earlier, he had written to me of his sadness at having to give up riding. Sitting atop his horse, Badger, he said, was when he felt most free; though Badger had earned a rest, it was with great reluctance that he would have to retire him. I answered that I hoped having to forfeit his greatest freedom would not lead him to follow in Badger's hoofsteps. My reply was greeted with an assurance that he would not throw in the towel just yet. As to his loss of freedom, his only comment was, "I think I'll get the surgeons to remove my legs at the hip and put me on wheels - that ought to do the trick".

It is with resistance, with a mixture of extreme gratitude and indescribable sadness - the kind that leaves you paralysed - that I offer this personal reflection. The most difficult part is to call up from memory the experiences of most significance, because there are so many of them.

I had laughed and laboured beside Walter daily for fifteen of the most important and formative years of my life. He was always there for each and every one of us. There was no special treatment - no favouritism.

When I wondered out loud if one could ever survive financially as an Alexander teacher, he said, "Well, you'll never get rich, but you will get tremendous existential satisfaction". That encouragement has never failed me whatever professional challenges have threatened.

In those years, it was my task to take Walter his beloved mug of tea at eleven each morning. One morning I made his tea and a cup for myself. I delivered Walter's to him in his room, and took mine to drink in the hall outside. I was chatting with some people, not particularly paying attention to my use. I put the mug up to my mouth – lurching my head forward to take a sip. The next moment I felt a large, warm hand close gently around my neck and delicately draw my neck back and up, and a gentle voice said, "That's better". It was Walter, of course. To this day I cannot drink anything without feeling that big hand on my neck – and to my knowledge, I have never since pulled down while drinking.

Brick, Walter's wartime navigator, has spoken powerfully of Walter's "coherent field of consciousness". I recall one occasion when I stood quietly in the doorway observing everybody working in the big teaching room. I was just taking a short break as I was feeling a little jaded after a full morning's teaching. All of a sudden I felt my body lengthen and widen, my breathing expand all on its own and an indescribable lightness fill me from head to foot. I was quite astounded at first because I was quite sure I had not generated this sudden charge myself. Then I felt a disturbance some distance behind me. I turned on my heels in surprise. There was nobody else near – only Walter standing some six feet away, grinning from ear to ear and focussing his attention on me. He was taking me up from a distance – generating so much upward direction that it reached out across the room and took me out of my tired collapse – not a hand in sight. I burst out laughing and said, "My God it's you. I can feel that from here!" He just kept grinning.

Though I now reside in Australia, and Walter is no longer with us, his energy remains nonetheless with me. Fortunately the computer had made it possible for me to remain the beneficiary of his constant verbal encouragement – which led me finally to start a small training course of my own and to attempt to pass on the torch with which he had lit up our lives.

Ron Murdock

When my son Andrew was about twelve, I asked Walter if he thought he could give Andrew some lessons and, of course, Walter agreed. Having Down's Syndrome, Andrew had trouble with his pelvis and legs – the right leg turned out at the hip quite severely.

Andrew took the lessons very seriously and told me firmly to wait in the waiting room while he had his time with Walter. However, one day Andrew asked me to come in with him, which I did. I sat very quietly behind Walter while he worked on Andrew in the chair. And, of course, in no time, Walter had Andrew going up and widening, and flowing in and out of the chair as easy as anything.

After taking Andrew in and out of the chair a few more times, Walter, with his right hand still on Andrew's neck to keep it free and lengthened, peered around to look at Andrew. Walter looked at Andrew with that wonderful smile of his, full of love and warmth, and said, "There you are, Andrew. That's who you really are. When people see you go down the street they'll say, *There goes Andrew*".

The lesson was over. Walter patted him on the back and said, "Jolly good, my dear". Andrew floated out of the room with the biggest grin on his face you can imagine.

This was one of those "light bulb" moments for me. I've never forgotten Walter's words and how, for me, they really sum up what the Alexander Technique is all about. It IS about bringing us and our pupils back to who we really are, so that when people see us go down the street they know, without a shadow of doubt, who they are seeing. More importantly, when WE go down the street, WE know who we are.

For someone like me who was abandoned at birth and spent the first seven months of life in an abusive orphanage, being in Walter's hands and feeling, finally, who I really am is what has given my life meaning and purpose and focus.

Jerry Sontag

I knew Walter's voice better than I knew him in person. Over the past 15 years, I saw Walter about a week each year. But when he agreed to let me do a book project compiling and editing some of his talks to trainees, I got a chance to listen to him for hours and hours and hours. Those times of listening to him on tape and editing his talks into a readable form were some of the most educational moments I have ever spent in my Alexander career. What struck me in listening to these short talks (and then reading and re-reading them after the talks came out in book form) was how clearly he saw the problems facing him, and how much confidence he had that the problems could be addressed. No easy answers. No quick fixes. Just a confidence that, in the long run, we had the tools to start looking at ways of changing ourselves.

I had many remarkable lessons with Walter, but one stands out. *Thinking Aloud* had just been published, and I came to London soon after that to study with Walter and celebrate the publication of his book. He was pleased with the book, which pleased me enormously. When I went in for my lesson, Walter started working and talking about the book and other thoughts that crossed his mind. It was a fantastic lesson, and it went on and on and on. That in and of itself was remarkable, because Walter, at least in my experience, was extremely punctual. I realized that he was giving me a double lesson as a way of saying thanks for the work I had put into the book. I almost told him it wasn't necessary, but I thought, *Who am I to refuse a gift so kindly given*?

When the lesson finally ended, I looked at my watch. Exactly half-an-hour had passed - not a moment more. Time had stretched luxuriously.

I miss him.

Steven Hallmark

Back in the late seventies I lived on a narrow boat on the canal. Every now and then it occurred to me that the rhythm of living on that boat was a bit like it must have been 120-150 years previously. I don't know what hours they worked then or what loads they transported, but the time it took to get from one place to another could not have changed much since the 1800's.

In the autumn of 1980 I took my boat from Birmingham to London to start my training at the Constructive Teaching Centre. It took a week, on my own. This was quite quick, I was told later. (By car I believe it takes about two or three hours.)

I look back with some astonishment on one memory of my training. Particularly in my private lessons, Walter would put a hand on the back of my neck and sort of knead and twitch it. It was very clear, though unsaid, that there was no question of me changing if I did not want to. Nothing need happen. It did not matter how much time it took, nothing need happen.

How astonishing, as I look back on it, that I was being taught by a man of such enormous renown, held in great esteem by his colleagues, at the place I thought of as being the best of its kind in the world, and nothing had to happen. This went on for the best part of a year! It took me into a new realm of time.

But why didn't he lose patience?

I can only suppose, in the light of later experience - and of the experience of how quick it had been to get to London in a week - that Walter lived in a time world of his own understanding, in which he was quite content. This meant that patience was unnecessary. He must have thought it was OK for me to take my time. That was a gift and an education. His time world was surely based on his experience of the time certain things take - you know, in the adverts it used to say you could get big muscles in a week - but nervous systems? Beliefs? Attitudes? Fears?

How can you be happy that it takes a whole week to get from Birmingham to London? But you are.

One very cold winter's day, Walter had to go out and had brought the car from the basement garage, but because the incline to the road was icy, the wheels could not get enough grip, and the car kept slipping back.

So Walter came back into the house, and asked some of the fellows on the training course to come outside and push the car up the slope.

Well, about six of us went outside, and took up positions at the back of the car. We, of course, were making sure we were giving our directions, and as Walter got back into the car, slipped it into gear, and let out the clutch, we started pushing, but not much happened!

So Walter wound down the window, looked back at us and said, "For God's sake, stiffen your necks and PUSH!!"

Steven Hallmark

Walter, I think, had a very advanced sense of the absurd. I loved this quality; after all we are only getting ourselves to do things we might be doing if we were not so interfered with. There was an occasion when Walter was asked, "How do you know when your neck is free?" It was of course a good question, and Walter, judging by the time he took to answer, was clearly deeply respectful of the questioner. Then he replied, "Well, you can move your head".

There must be something of the genius in that. It has been said (by Montessori amongst others) that genius consists of observing things which everyone ought to be able to see but can't.

Elizabeth Langford

I remember that, during my training, Walter once drew my attention to the extremely delicate movement he was suggesting to someone's head. He likened the work of his fingers to something a violinist might do. I said, "Mm, yes..." somewhat doubtfully, because I was thinking naïvely, "But it doesn't have to *sound* exactly right, does it?" Walter didn't press the point – and now at last I understand what he was showing me.

Nanette Walsh

Over the last several years I periodically had the opportunity to see Walter for an extended series of lessons. They were sheer joy. His hands, like his gentle laugh, seamlessly but firmly coaxing me out of interferences just at the edge of my consciousness – I had not yet imagined the refined and lasting unity that Walter consistently brought forth. His invitation to greater strength and stability in my back continued to surface long after each lesson ended; it was palpable, and it would have taken real determination to refuse. Still, the choice was mine, as it always was with Walter.

One day in particular I arrived after reading another teacher's writings about FM's training course and the period after his death. It contained several portrayals of events that were at odds with my own research at the time. (I had been working for some time on a book about another first generation teacher.) Moreover, it contained passages that often portrayed Walter in what I found to be a surprisingly patronizing manner. I was so dismayed to see things in print that ran counter to my knowledge and experience, that I must have arrived at my lesson in a pretty heightened state of confusion. When I asked him what he thought of it all, he quietly and kindly said, "Well, my dear, writing like this demonstrates how idiosyncratic memory really is". That was it: memory is idiosyncratic. There would be no rebuttal, no counter judgment, and no indignation – just a generous observation of a very human condition in which he undoubtedly included himself.

In one simple statement, he cut away the root of my anxiety, taught me something terribly important about the reading and writing of personal memoirs, and brought my focus back to the present moment and the business of the lesson – namely that of taking responsibility for myself in the face of this very fallible human condition. While his hands gently invited me to quieten down and free up, his simple statement contained a further invitation: an invitation to greater maturity, greater responsibility, greater conscience and greater trust. Really, it was an unspoken but firm invitation to greater faith.

Yes, faith: personal and individual and rooted in the senses. For the record, I never heard Walter use the word. I doubt he would have. Just as I never heard him use the word humility; he simply lived it. Occasionally he talked about the gradual development of "confidence born of experiences". Experiences during which he would every so often gently cajole me along: "There is nothing to do – all you have to want is to be free – nothing to do – you don't need to watch yourself – I am watching you – you are looking for freedom..." I felt so cared for and supported under his watchful hands that faith and its promise of persistence steadily took root, and the possibility of freedom did not seem so unattainable or frightening.

At the Refresher Course last summer, and again at the Oxford Congress, Walter suggested that we ask ourselves two questions. One: Where am I? Two: Where do I want to go? He went on to say, "Of course, as a human being you balance on two feet, and no matter where you are going, you are first going up! So stop a bit, realize your surroundings. Once you know where you are, you know where up is – you know the direction you are going. That is where you want to go! That is where you need to go".

These two questions, and the potent desire they point to, are for me now as they were then a wonderful distillation of Walter's patient invitation to faith in the individual and the inherent freedom therein: never a demand - always an invitation - purely issued from his own ground of imperfect being - perfectly grounded in the practical experience of inhibition and direction.

At the close of one day of the Refresher Course last summer Walter stood smiling quietly near the door while he cast a glance about the room looking to see that everyone had received their turn from him. The glance was perfunctory rather than necessary; Walter never missed anyone. When no one came forward, his remarkable smile turned into an easy roll of laughter as he bid us goodbye, "Then - I shall love you - and leave you".

His leaving now final - his patient invitation remains.

Alex Murray

It is impossible to epitomize forty-seven years of friendship in a couple of anecdotes. Walter was a remarkable man, most generous with his time (in the early days, he would give a demonstration without charge). He was scrupulously fair in all his dealings - even with his critics - and a pillar of support to the many who relied on him.

It was through Walter that Joan and I became friends of Frank and Helen Jones, and of Raymond and Marjorie Dart. His benevolent influence will continue to inspire those who came into contact with him.

Pearl Ausubel

Long before I ever met Walter and before I was involved in the Alexander Technique, I heard of the "miracle" he had performed. I lived away from New York City, much involved in husband, children and faculty affairs, and saw my sister Judy (Judith Leibowitz) for short visits, perhaps twice in a year. The Alexander Technique was in the periphery of my consciousness but the "miracle" that Mr. Carrington wrought was brought to the center. Mr. Carrington had Judy climbing stairs by herself.

But Judy couldn't climb stairs!

A severe case of polio when she was fifteen had left her with no normal muscles from the waist down. She needed a railing to pull herself up even one step.

The "miracle" was to climb a few stairs by herself without a railing. Walter's hands giving directions helped her to "float up the stairs".

How did he do this? No one else, not F.M. Alexander himself, had ever given her such an experience. She never forgot the wonder of floating up a few stairs.

I don't know if this happened at other times when she visited Walter in London. However, the memory of that experience was so vivid that she had a small staircase built for teaching purposes that went up one side and down the other. In this way, she could recreate for her students her experience of lightness.

Thea Kreft

I arrived in London at the School from Cape Town, South Africa 14 days after my youngest child, Peter, had died suddenly in a motorbike accident at the age of 20.

Looking back, I think I was not quite there and felt very sorry for myself. Walter and Dilys were very kind to me.

I had been there for a while. Walter, each time he gave me a turn, would give a little impulse with his middle finger under my ribcage and I did not know why he did that. Until...

One day, I got my turn and again he gave that little shove under the right side of the ribcage. There was a surprising reaction. Out of nowhere I felt as if a huge iron band around my ribcage had burst or exploded and a flood of tears, like a river that had been held back, issued forth.

Walter realised what had happened and let me leave the room for some privacy. He did not say much. (Well, what can one say?)

Of course, all the time he had encouraged my very contracted diaphragm to release – with success. For me it was a real "Aha" experience.

Meredith Page

Walter had an authority, neither dominance nor forcefulness, but an inner authority which had grown in him over a lifetime working on himself. He had deep compassion for human frailty yet never pitted himself against it. Instead, he understood what it is that leads to real change and growth and he spent his life investigating and practising it. He simply knew. With neither mystical pretensions nor any particular belief, he showed us that the more concrete and down-to-earth our work is, the more infused with spirit it becomes.

Whenever I think of him, I am reminded of those wonderful words of the philosopher Martin Buber:

"What do we expect when we are in despair, and yet go to a man? Surely a presence, by means of which we are told that, nevertheless, there is meaning."

Don Kirkley

Here are my two fondest memories:

The first one is of a lesson during my second or third year of my course at Lansdowne Road in the mid-1980's. I was having my termly private lesson with Walter and had been standing there patiently in front of the chair while Walter did whatever he did behind me. After what seemed like a considerable time, perhaps five minutes, I became quite angry, saying to myself, "If he is so bloody good, why isn't anything happening?" This mounting feeling of frustration and anger lasted a few seconds before I suddenly changed tack and almost burst into tears. Walter poked his head round the side of me and enquired, "Everything all right Don?" Oh yes, Walter, absolutely fine.

Several years after finishing my training, I was having a private lesson. Walter had been working on me for some time and then initiated the movement from sitting to standing with the minutest pressure on my head. I then found myself rising from the chair as if drawn upwards by an invisible force that was completely outside my control. All inhibition and knowledge of the Technique deserted me and I turned my head, while continuing to rise like a slow motion rocket, to see what on earth it was behind me that was causing this strange effect. I remember expecting an elaborate apparatus of strings and pulleys but there was only Walter with a rather resigned but faintly exasperated look on his face.

Walter's skill was astonishingly subtle. On the training course, I often saw him get someone so beautifully balanced and light that he could then take them in and out of the chair several times in quick succession, using just one finger somewhere on the person's back.

The delighted expression of the student and the happy laughter of the onlookers are a vivid memory. I used to think Walter challenged himself day by day to achieve that state of easy balance for different students. I think I know how it worked, but I haven't yet seen anyone else bring students to such confident nonchalance.

For years, I used to take every opportunity of watching Walter working on other people, as I tried to get an idea of what was happening. There were always fascinating changes to be seen in any student or teacher he had his hands on – but whatever Walter himself was about, it usually seemed too subtle for observation. Then, I made a point of watching *him* more than his pupil. I can't say it got much easier! But I saw clearly, as they walked away, how each pupil got the total effect of his work on them.

Some years ago, I visited Walter with a couple of my own students; I had asked him to help them put their hands on me. I was seated. Walter had just put a student into monkey. He then placed the student's hands on my head, so lightly that they were barely touching it. Walter then came behind me and gently put his own hand on the back of my neck, as he had so often done in the past.

I continued to sit there and direct, waiting to see how he would proceed with the student.

Suddenly I found myself in a standing position, with no awareness of any of the three of us having done anything whatsoever. Twenty-odd years as an Alexander teacher had not prepared me for that, and I exclaimed, "Who did what?" Walter appeared faintly irritated - just as Don describes - and said, "Well, of course I initiated it". The student said that at a certain moment he had felt a heightened sense of responsibility for continuing in his good monkey. In retrospect, I remembered having felt an infinitesimal lengthening of one of Walter's fingers on my neck.

We didn't discuss it, but I suppose Walter's air of slight irritation was because I really ought not to have been so surprised to find that "the right thing does itself".

Jane Aaronson

I was born with the condition spina bifida, for which I was operated on the day of my birth. Three weeks later, I was diagnosed as having hydrocephalus. I was not expected to live. A further unusual operation was performed, but medical opinion was still doubtful if I would have more than a vegetable-like existence. My parents did everything possible to find out all the options.

At four years old, I was still unable to sit up. From that age until my mid-twenties, I had Alexander lessons regularly – at first with F.M. Alexander himself, but he died when I had had only about three weeks of lessons, and his assistants were left to continue what he had begun. I was lucky to have lessons from Walter Carrington, and these continued for many years.

At Lansdowne Road, as well as my private lessons with Walter, I had lessons in term time in the large training room, where several other teachers, supervised by Walter, worked simultaneously on me, while I sat on a toy donkey. (Among the teachers were Peggy Williams and Joan Murray.) It was only after Walter's death that I learnt that he had later devised what came to be known as *saddle work*: a way of working on people's legs that originated in my lessons on that historic donkey. (Walter tells the story in his book *Personally Speaking*.)

By the time I was about thirteen, thanks to the Technique, my upper body had become quite strong, and I was introduced to callipers and crutches. I learnt to use the crutches with Walter's help. The way was now open to an independent life as an adult - going to university, driving a car, having my own flat, and earning a living.

Walter and Dilys were always very kind to me. I remember particularly that they visited me regularly to give me lessons when I was at boarding school. I had difficulty in writing, and Walter helped me with that. I looked on Walter and Dilys as an uncle and aunt, and those weekend visits were the highlight of my life. To say I am still grateful would be an absurd understatement.

Jane says I probably remember more than she does - after all, she was a child, and her Alexander lessons were just part of her daily life at the time. She couldn't know how interested we all were - teachers and students - in her progress. She was about twelve when I first knew her and it was impressive to see her in her wheelchair: by then, her upper body didn't suggest any handicap.

I was privileged to witness the first time Jane felt anything in her leg: Edward Gellatly touched her foot lightly when she couldn't see what he was doing. She looked like someone listening carefully for a distant sound. "It's my left foot, isn't it?" she said. "You're doing something like this with your fingers." Soon she was complaining about bumps and bruises that she would not have noticed before.

A particular memory is of Jane - at about sixteen - inviting me to dinner when her parents were out. A good hostess, she sent me into the sitting room while she made the coffee. Responding to a shout from the kitchen, I was amazed to see her perched on the worktop, after finding the coffee grains on a high shelf. "How on earth did you get up there?" I asked. Jane - who couldn't use leg power to *jump* up - explained carefully, "It is quite easy if you free your neck and send your head forward and up." (!) I tried but the worktop was too high for me - and Jane is quite a lot shorter than me. I remember thinking she had understood more about the application of the Alexander Technique than most people ever do.

Now in her fifties, Jane said the other day, "I still try to live the Technique as much as possible." (E. Langford)

Elizabeth Langford

A few years ago, in a private lesson, Walter asked me a riddle:

"Do you know the difference between a doctor and God the Father?"

"No, Walter, I give it up. What is the difference?"

"God doesn't think he's a doctor."

Jean Clark

Walter's influence on my life began even before I met him. For sixteen years, since I left school, I worked on insects at the Natural History Museum in London. In 1965, a new member of staff joined our section: a girl of nineteen with beautiful long, red hair. You wouldn't readily have associated her with a museum, and in fact she was a former beauty queen. Unfortunately, our new colleague suffered from recurring lower back pain. Hospital investigations and X-rays had revealed nothing that needed medical attention, and the only advice was "bed rest when the pain is bad".

The head of our section was keenly interested in something called the Alexander Technique, which he said could be beneficial for many seemingly disparate problems. This sounded far-fetched to his young colleague, but eventually he persuaded her to see a man in Holland Park. The following day (while we were standing beside the beautiful mahogany cabinets that then housed the named parasite wasp collections) I asked her a question that changed my life. "How did you get on with your Alexander session?" She said that "this man" (who of course turned out to be Walter) had told her that her lower back pain was coming from her neck. She lifted her long, flowing red hair, and, from side view, showed me an incredible distortion in her neck vertebrae, which stuck out at an angle, like a stair. She considered it ugly, so concealed it with her hair, and the hospital had only X-rayed her lower back, never looking at her neck.

Even I could appreciate that a misalignment at the top of the spine could adversely affect the spine lower down. I was impressed that "this man", who apparently had no medical training, had spotted something that doctors had overlooked. She had further lessons with Walter and no longer took sick leave because of her back.

The head of our section was delighted, but not surprised. Sensing that my curiosity had been aroused, he suggested that I might have some lessons with his wife, who had recently trained with Walter at Lansdowne Road. After those first lessons I attended a series of small evening classes given by Walter and some of his assistants. At ten shillings a session it was good value for money! I began to think of a career change.

I visited another training course where the hours fitted more conveniently with a part-time job. However, I was a shy girl in those days; Walter's benign manner put me at my ease and I felt that his was the more suitable training atmosphere for me. At that time (1966) the class was small – it was even contemplated that it might soon have to close – but the tide turned and we soon grew to eleven students.

I look back on those three years as halcyon days in which seemingly not much happened – but everything happened. Whoever you were, whatever your background, Walter could make a link with you. Thank you, Walter, for showing me how to find myself and my life's work.

Neil Schapera

I think of Walter with great affection as a man with a superb sense of humor - slightly dry, intelligent humor that was extremely funny. His matter-of-fact delivery, the twinkle in his eyes, and his occasional chuckle, were so endearing, and hugely entertaining. Nothing was a surprise to him; he would comment to someone's description of a very peculiar behavior or incident, "Well, of course".

I loved Walter's talks, expressions of his unmatched experience and wisdom, and sprinkled with the funniest anecdotes and perspicacious comments. Such as these:

"The reason why people habitually stiffen being their desire to avoid 'punishing collisions with the earth'."

"There have to be alternative ways of doing various acts without pulling down. If not – these acts must be given up."

"Feelings about oneself can be just as habitual as any mechanical process."

"The desire to stiffen (neck) muscles should be inhibited as a preliminary. It's not the stiffening but the desire to stiffen. We're not concerned with the muscles but with the thought process."

"The core of the Technique lies in not doing what you don't want to do."

Nothing seemed to faze Walter on the training course; his consistent skills of inhibition and avoidance of unproductive engagement were remarkable to witness. Some people wished for a more personal response from him to their problems, but they didn't realize he was in fact giving a most personal response: that of consciously chosen inhibition. For he knew that his refraining from engagement – while still expressing understanding – was going to be in the very best interests of the person in front of him.

I loved his lessons, his constant light conversation, and tantalizing anecdotes about F.M. Alexander that – with Walter's passing – are gone forever.

"FM used to get annoyed if one asked 'how are you?' For one thing people don't know, and for another, it's bad to invite them to consider it."

FM had made good contact with a Rev. Penniman - "They'd ride and drink together – the rides and wine terminated when Penniman told FM that he'd had discussions with Jesus recently."

"FM said that the main way of getting over nervousness and apprehension is to stop fussing about whether you are right or wrong."

During the lessons, Walter would talk about how "some people" have this or that misuse pattern which he would casually describe, and it was some time before I caught on that this was his most kind and non-startle-provoking way of informing me of my own patterns of misuse.

What a wonderful man! I am left with great sadness, and immeasurable appreciation.

Elizabeth Langford

Walter was only fourteen years older than I was, yet his style was rather that of my father's generation: the collar and tie, the three-piece suit, the tweeds at weekends. Conventional, you might have said.

But you couldn't faze Walter. In the "swinging sixties", a woman student made an experiment, to see if it could be done. I happened to be in the entrance hall when she arrived at the (very good but rather sedate) Lansdowne Road annual party, her male escort wearing an exquisite long-skirted evening frock of emerald green brocade! Walter didn't blink as he gave his usual warm greeting: "My dear chap, how nice to see you. Let me pour you a glass of wine."

No, you couldn't faze Walter.

Robin Möckli

I was just twenty when I began my training at Lansdowne Road, young, scattered, and impatient. I found it very difficult to integrate the work with the end-gaining and intellectual education I had undergone until that time. One day in a private lesson I burst out, "Oh Walter, don't you ever get bored with this work?"

There was an already familiar pause, which meant that my question was going to be treated more seriously than I had anticipated, that I wasn't going to be able to trick him into a hasty or frivolous remark.

"Well my dear," he began, his right hand continuing relentless elasticizing work on my back, "I had quite enough excitement during the war you know, and when it was over I only wanted one thing, to be back here and to do this work".

At this point I knew nothing about Walter's wartime heroism; he was much too modest to ever talk about this without precise questioning, and his answer had already given me quite enough to think about. That there was more to Walter than met the eye began to be more palpable. The idea that war, which I had always viewed as something entirely negative, could have this positive effect of concentrating the mind, made me begin to examine some of the things I accepted as givens. That it was possible to have just one basic wish, and not be blown hither and thither by various half-wishes as I felt myself to be, was also food for thought.

Of course this wasn't the sort of answer I'd expected or wanted, but it was very typical of Walter's way of fielding questions. You got an honest answer, but also a good dose of something that it would be useful for you to think about. Like the blind men with the elephant, I felt as though I was fiddling around with the trunk in the dark and he was describing the rest of the animal to me. It was disconcerting, but it was also exciting, and I spent a lot of time working out what questions to ask from that time on. Yet I still wish I had asked more and had written down more of his answers.

After about a year on the training course I was asked to take over the secretarial work. I was young, inexperienced and lacking in self-confidence, and to this day I do not know if Walter and Dilys asked me because they thought I'd be good at it or because they wanted to keep an eye on me. As an American, I was completely unversed in the art of brewing an English cup of tea; the intervening years have mercifully erased from my memory what tasteless concoction might have been passed off as tea in our home. Yet Walter bravely accepted a cup from me every day without complaint. Then one morning I was called to the phone and let the tea stew for at least twice as long as I normally did. It looked very black and murky to me, but there was no time to do anything about it, so down to Walter's teaching room it went. After the next lesson was finished he beamed at me with his great warm smile: "That was a really good cup of tea!" I must have visibly blanched at the thought of the predecessors to this at last successful cup; and then I'm sure I also smiled, for who could do otherwise when confronted with a beaming Walter. This was so typical also of his teaching style: simply let people get on with things and give them encouragement when necessary, no words wasted.

Walter would tell us this at least once a year while I was training (from '91 to '94). He would say:

Shall I tell you what I do when a little child comes for lessons?

I ask, "Do you know the magic word?"

The child, after thinking a little while, will say, "No".

Then I say, "Right! That's the magic word."

Elizabeth Langford

In 1966, when I joined the training course, Walter used to end the morning by giving a thirty-minute lesson to one or other of us, while the whole class watched and listened to his remarks.

I remember vividly the first time Walter gave me a turn in front of everybody. It was during my first term, and apart from the awful state I was in when I started my training, I had been up till 4 a.m. with a close friend who - at my suggestion - had just begun to have Alexander lessons. He was emerging from a really bad time, and was then going through a highly argumentative stage. Of course, I didn't yet know enough about the Technique to answer him. I said so, but that didn't help: he was pretty upset and we just went round in circles. In the circumstances, it was not easy next morning to sit facing my haggard reflection in that big wall mirror!

During the next half-hour, Walter kept finding different ways of saying the same thing: "Wherever you are going, there's only one place you can start from, and that's the place where you are."

In a way, it was rather hard to take, but as we left the room I heard a teacher say, "What a marvellous lesson!"

Yes indeed - forty years on, I think of it every day.

Wherever you are going, you can only start from where you are.

Jill Payne

I trained at Lansdowne Road 1999-2002 and when I had visited the school Walter had been out on one of his riding days. My first meeting with him was a lesson I had while waiting to start the course. I was a little nervous as the great man ushered me into his study.

"So, my dear," he said "you're thinking of training with us?" I nodded. "Well, you've probably been told to free your neck, and let your head go forward and up, and all that sort of thing - well I want you to forget all about that and just look out of the window."

Responding to his gentle touch I relaxed and started to go up and then Walter said warmly, "There you see; it's money for old rope!"

Walter's ability to demystify the work and put people at their ease will always stay with me.

Joe Armstrong

The most meaningful and powerful thing that Walter said to me was in a private lesson during the time I was on the teacher training course at Lansdowne Road (1969-72). I can't remember what the general subject of our conversation was that day, but we were obviously discussing the broader implications for humanity of Alexander's discoveries, rather than the usual nuts and bolts of how to get on with daily living that Walter was so superb at talking you through. It has certainly guided me in a fundamental way through my living and teaching over the last thirty-odd years.

Walter said:
You know, Joe, I don't give too much thought to religion and spiritual things, but I DO think there is such a thing as "the human spirit."

To me, too, that's what the Alexander Work is really about: the evolution of the human spirit.

Brian Dodgeon

I trained at Lansdowne Road from 1994 to '97, and have been a weekly visitor since then, putting hands on the students and often chatting with Walter on Friday afternoons.

I remember one of the most concise and satisfying replies Walter gave to a difficult question was when asked how you could sum up the difference between somebody who's "going up" and somebody who's "pulling down" Walter said, "Well, it's like the difference between a hovercraft that's switched on, and one that's not".

He often talked, of course, about the fact that people often stop breathing momentarily just as they're about to do a tricky movement like bending to get something out of a fridge, which then causes them to tighten. In explaining the value of keeping the breathing going nicely whilst doing an action, he'd say, "Otherwise, it's like putting your handbrake on just as you're about to drive off".

There was also a charming little limerick he used to recite (I think this was in the context of discussing the concept of faulty sensory appreciation!):

There was a faith-healer from Deal,
Who said, "Although pain isn't real,
If I sit on a pin,
And it punctures my skin,
I dislike what I fancy I feel."

I remember a quote of FM's which Walter recounted to me once:
FM was asked in an interview whether he felt he had really done something for posterity over his long career, and he replied, "What's posterity ever done for me?"

And when handing out beautifully printed certificates at graduation ceremonies, Walter was fond of pointing out how much things had changed since he graduated in 1939. FM had instructed him to type the certificate out himself, using his own discretion as to the wording, and then FM signed it.

Leah Landau

I had my first lesson with Walter on the training course at Lansdowne Road in 1983. I remember a feeling of wholeness and lightness afterwards and was amazed at how skilfully he worked on me.

I was 28 years old and had just graduated from University where I had been studying English Literature as a "mature student". During my Finals I had got myself into a terrible state of tension and to counteract that Walter said, "If at first you don't succeed, give up and go home!"- very good advice to a hard-working, ambitious intellectual.

In another lesson we discussed my Jewish background and Walter referred me to the Bible, where God said the Israelites were a "stiff-necked people" - we both roared with laughter over this but it did help me to stop being so stubborn and consider freeing my neck as a new possibility.

It was hard for me to give up end-gaining and I was worried I would lose all motivation and never achieve anything again. Some time during my second year I began to understand a little bit about inhibition and direction. I felt completely happy and at times blissful continuously for about ten days. I had a new experience of lightness and freedom, and of being able to breathe - which was new to me, as I habitually held my breath.

I think some of my fellow students thought I had gone a bit mad - all full of love and light - but Walter was completely unfazed by the whole episode and seemed to accept it all as normal.

Towards the end of my third year, I had a blinding flash of inspiration and said to Walter that for me inhibition was the same thing as directing. That is, if I could truly stop, then the direction would happen by itself. He did not agree or disagree, but said that if that worked for me it was a valid idea.

I will always be grateful to Walter for giving me the feeling and the assurance that I was all right. He showed real compassion and acceptance and let me know that I was whole and healed - mirroring to me a state of perfection where life is all right and I am all right. Hopefully I have managed to teach in the same spirit although I think you have to be enlightened to not judge people at all!

About half way through my training, I observed one night that as I started to fall asleep, I reverted to my pre-AT posture. So I said, "No" to my misuse, and was instantly wide awake. This kept happening for much of the night and for almost a week until, fortunately, it was my turn to have a private lesson with Walter. I told him about it and he quite simply suggested that I needed my sleep and "should allow yourself to sleep, however bad the misuse is, and sort yourself out when you wake up in the morning".

Wisdom is so simple sometimes, isn't it?

Ron Murdock

Visiting student: Walter, since I've been on the training course, I have had a lot of depression. What should I do?

Walter (with his usual smile): Well, you see my dear, it's like this. Some days when I get up and look out of the window, I say to myself: "It's raining." And it is.

Jeanne Day

My first day on the Training Course:

Jeanne: Walter, I am surprised that the students here look as awkward as anyone else.

Walter: No reason to be surprised – you see, everybody, every one of us is to some degree spastic.

spastic – (physiological term) means "performing involuntary contractile movements" (Shorter Oxford English Dictionary)

Sara Solnick

The memory I have of Walter that I would like to share, is of my first group lesson with him in my fifth term of training at Lansdowne Road. I couldn't wait to be in the afternoon class, because it meant that finally I was going to be able to work with Walter.

On the first day of term I arrived early. I knew he gave private lessons at 11 a.m., and I was not going to join the ranks of the sad and remorseful who had managed to miss one of their precious lessons. I looked at the list in the teaching room and duly noted that my first Walter lesson was not due for some weeks. At 11.30 a.m. someone came in and asked if anyone would like an extra Walter group, as someone had failed to turn up. Well, unable to believe my good fortune, I was across that hall and into his room in a flash - no inhibition there then.

Walter, who I thought did not know me at all, greeted me by name and asked me to stand by the chair. He was standing behind the upright chair, with his right hand on the top left-hand edge of it. I remember thinking, "Well, if he's standing on the left, then I had better be on the right, so I won't be in his way".

Our group of three was complete, though I have to admit that I have no recollection at all of who the others were. I was standing by the chair, another pupil was in front of the chair, and someone else was sitting observing. Walter asked me whether I normally liked to work from that side. Alarm bells rang in my head, but I really had no idea what I normally did; I was totally confused, so I just said "Yes". Walter quietly moved round to my side of the chair to stand next to me and put a hand on, and I suddenly realised my error. "Help! What to do next?" I couldn't think at all.

He then asked me to take myself into monkey. "Monkey? Monkey! How on earth do you take yourself into monkey?" By now I was in a state of total panic, my palms sweating, my heart racing, and no thought of inhibition or anything else in my mind. I made a total hash of moving my "pupil" into and out of the chair, and then I sat and watched as the next person went to stand on the left of the chair and seamlessly manoeuvre their pupil.

I had a second chance to work during the group, and Walter just said, indicating to the left, "Would you prefer to work from here this time?"

Well, I suppose I made a pretty awful mess of that first group, but I certainly learnt a few things. Walter gave me the opportunity to think about what I wanted to do and how to proceed, but in my excitement at working with him, and my desperation to impress, I gave myself no time whatsoever to stop and consider the means whereby I might achieve this. I allowed feeling to dictate; I didn't listen to what Walter said, and I wasted my first, and long-awaited, opportunity. But Walter never said anything about it. He knew, for sure, that I was a useless bundle of nerves, and maybe wondered what on earth I was doing in his group at all, but then maybe he was used to people going to pieces in his presence.

So, not only did Walter not humiliate me or reprimand me in any way, but he also left me alone to realise, in time, what I had done through my lack of any conscious control. He knew of course, that I would learn so much better if I could use the experience to work it out for myself. If he had pointed out my error to me directly, he would have been doing what he always warned us to avoid: "making a bad situation worse," and I was quite capable of doing that all by myself!

I learnt a very big lesson that day, and I will never forget it.

Dinah Goodes

I can recall many memorable moments from my training with Walter but these recollections stand out for me at this time.

As a student from Australia I always felt that, having come so far, I must get the most from the training that I could and so rarely missed days. However, one year I very much wanted to go to the Chelsea Flower Show; and by my last year I was thoroughly addicted to the tennis at Wimbledon, watched on TV. I told Walter before taking odd days off why I would be absent each time and he responded jovially, "Good for you! Enjoy it!" What better indulgence could you ask for?

My last memory is one that comes back to me the most often. It pervades my own teaching over ten years later.

Once or twice a week we would have "group" with Walter, a half-hour spent, usually in threes, learning how to "put hands on". This fundamental action contains the seeds of the whole technique for a teacher. Walter stood to the side, his walking stick in one hand, a fully focussed but widely conscious presence, as we repeated the same motions week in, week out - with minute, incremental changes. However, benign as he was, Walter could quietly make a sharp comment every now and then, to nudge you along your psychophysical way.

This was where you came into your own as a teacher and a human being and learnt the Alexander Technique. I cherish this memory of Walter particularly because that was real teaching and it is rare. Thank you, Walter.

Elizabeth Langford

Mention of Wimbledon reminds me of the day teachers and students kept sneaking upstairs to watch the – now legendary – match between Connors and Gonzales. At one point there were more of us around the TV in the Carringtons' flat than in the training course, but no complaint was made. Nor did I feel the need to apologize for absenting myself to see Teresa Berganza rehearse at Covent Garden. Enthusing about her singing, her acting, her co-ordination, I arrived late for afternoon class. No problem – Walter knew it was part of my education.

Susan Cohen

The garden of Lansdowne Road was a metaphor of my life with the Carringtons. As a seed is nourished into a bud and then into a flowering plant so was I encouraged to enter into a new world and ultimately into a profession that has enriched my life. No feature of the Carrington's home and school remains so vivid in my memory as the rear garden. No element of the training course stands out as prominently as the wisdom of Walter's daily lectures, his group and private lessons. When I think of the garden's tranquillity and beauty I recall Walter's quiet but dignified manner. The rich colors of the garden in Spring evoke memories of Walter's radiant smile and calm demeanor. The year in and year out consistency of how the garden would bloom paralleled the constancy of the "Carrington way". The fresh breezes that wafted through the rooms at 18 Lansdowne Road remind me of the laughter that Walter's jokes at the end of the day would evoke. (I have to admit that sometimes I failed to grasp Walter's very special humor, but eventually one of us would break out laughing. A ripple of laughter soon followed, and we would all end the day on a lighter note.) At one spot in the garden stood a white wooden bench that offered us solace from the school's rich and stimulating atmosphere. In much the same way Walter's private lessons would transport us into another world - one of utter presence. Even the lush pink roses resembled Walter's effervescent smile and boyish pink cheeks.

A quintessential English garden knows its own mind and proudly radiates beauty. Walter was a quintessential English gentleman in his dress, manner, speech, and style. His knowledge of the Technique, science, current affairs, and even dressage inspired us to enlarge our understanding of the world of Alexander and beyond.

And so dear Walter, with your big smile, your big heart and those wonderful big hands! I hope your departure leaves us all with uplifting Walter thoughts. May your spirit continue to soar.

It was Susan Cohen who kindly sent us the photo of the garden at Lansdowne Road, which appears on the back cover. (Ed.)

Ted Dimon

In 1983 I went to the Constructive Teaching Centre at Lansdowne Road in London to finish my training in the Alexander Technique with Walter and Dilys Carrington. Although it is now 22 years ago, the time I spent there, and what I learned, remains with me vividly to this day.

Walter Carrington was widely renowned for his experience and remarkable skill; he was also one of the most thoughtful teachers I have ever known. I was due to graduate from the training course in July. Anticipating going to graduate school the following fall, I was worried because I had always disliked writing by hand: in school, I would have to take a great deal of hand-written notes. I asked Walter if he could help me with this. He responded in his kind but detached way, saying that perhaps he could help. However, he said nothing about it in class during the days that followed. I went home for the weekend, thinking Walter had forgotten.

When I returned on Monday, the entire class gathered for "Games", the period when Walter would lead the class in a specific activity that everyone would then try out. He would typically demonstrate on someone picked at random, but this time he called me over from the far end of the room, and, in front of the group, proceeded to demonstrate in minute detail the mechanics of sitting, holding a pen, and writing, which he continued for a period of three days.

On another occasion I asked Walter a question. He said he would think it over. Again, after more than a week, I was convinced he had forgotten. Some days later I came into his office for my private lesson, and he began to tell a story. I didn't know at first what the point of the story was, until it slowly dawned on me that he was answering my question. Walter had that way. He would start to tell a story or describe some situation, and you couldn't imagine what he was talking about. As he went on, you realized he was indirectly talking about you, telling you, in the most non-confrontational way imaginable, something you needed to hear.

Walter was supportive, non-judgmental, and kind. He had the most powerful direction of any teacher I have ever worked with. He was also unusually perceptive and thoughtful. He thought about what was needed, even to the point that he would wait several days or a week to answer a question. And just when you thought he'd forgotten all about it, there he was, carefully answering your question and right to the point.

Walter Carrington wasn't just a good teacher; he embodied good teaching. He was brilliant with his hands, but he also cared, in exactly the right way. More than any teacher I have ever worked with, he maintained the kind of detachment that made it possible for you to learn. Most teachers try to teach you; Walter gave you room to learn.

And if you had a concern, he never forgot to tell you just the right story.

Elizabeth Langford

It was really impressive how quick Walter was in making associations - even over considerable gaps of time. As a schoolgirl, in the 1940's, I had appreciated a newspaper column by "Beachcomber", whose wit overflowed into fantasy, creating imaginary authorities such as "Mr Justice Cocklecarrot" and "Dr Strabismus (whom God preserve) of Utrecht". Some twenty years later, Walter was in the middle of explaining the similarity between Alexander's "Primary Control" and the "Zentralapparat" later described by Dr Rudolf Magnus of the University of Utrecht. As Walter pronounced Magnus's name, he caught my eye, and calmly added "whom God preserve", without interrupting his explanation.

Walter's memory and his alertness were truly amazing. He always seemed to know what was going on everywhere in the big teaching room. I noticed I had only to say, "I don't think I quite understand such-and-such" to get an explanation from Walter during the next few days. It often happened, even though my remark had been made to someone else and I didn't think he could possibly have heard it.

Jill Geiger

It is no easy task putting together words to express the love and respect I have for Walter and the influence he has had on me. One vivid memory I have of working with him took place during a brief turn while visiting the training course years ago. What he said at the time has left me but I recall his hand on my back as though it were still there. In that moment in the chair, his hand and his words made it quite clear that it was possible to really do nothing. The present moment opened up and there was all the time in the world.

Ever calm, accepting, respectful, thoughtful, good-humored and unhurried, Walter embodied the principles of our work. With his warm smile, he always met me at my level while offering a clear and irresistible invitation to come along with him and move effortlessly into the next moment by being fully aware in the present one. He was a truly great and wise man and my experiences of him will remain with me inspiring my being and my teaching.

Emma Hargreaves

I was blessed to train under Walter and Dilys's guidance from 1994 to 1996. Towards the end of the training I had a very memorable private lesson with Walter.

That particular day Walter spoke at length, his soft fleshy open hand, signing out its vibrant language on my upper back for most of the lesson. While the subject matter was interesting and relevant to this work, I confess I was a little uneasy that my precious half hour lesson was passing without once moving from the chair.

Referring to some students' keen interest in physical exercise, gym workouts, and the like, Walter said that so long as they kept time with a song, they would do less damage to themselves. "If they can't keep the singing going with relative ease, then they are definitely doing a lot of harm, that is, fixing their breathing and so on." He gave examples of African women singing as they worked and soldiers marching in time to rhythmic song – the body, he said, being energized by sound and rhythm. He mentioned the work of the Frenchman, Alfred Tomatis and his discoveries of how listening to certain frequencies energizes the brain and body.

When reading aloud, Walter suggested choosing something poetic, so the voice mechanism can be energized by the rhythm.

A light tap on my shoulder and Walter said, "There you go", which I knew to be the lesson end. At last I rose from the chair, the first time since arriving, and took my departure. It was not until crossing the corridor from Walter's room into the main teaching room that I received the revelation of the lesson.

Walter had awakened a lifeline of energy in my back beyond what had already happened during the training: the gift of a connection and buoyancy, given, so gently, so unassumingly under the hands of one who knows how to be empty.

Chyna Gordon

Being taught by Walter and Dilys Carrington between 1999-2002 was one of the most fulfilling and uplifting times of my life. I am honoured to have been taught at the Carrington school, and Walter you will be deeply missed.

Vivien Mackie

One day during my training, Walter had just dropped his hand on my neck to begin my daily "turn", when the electrician came in and asked Walter where he wanted the new switches in the next room. Walter said "Excuse me, my dear", leaving his hand where it was, while he talked to the electrician.

Meanwhile Direction was coming through at about a million volts. I felt I had ALL of Walter's attention. I expect the electrician was quite satisfied with the attention he got. Little did he know.

Gwyneth Lloyd

I spent a term with Walter Carrington to finish my South African training course in 1985. There are many aspects of his work which are absolutely unique. I can still feel the care in his hands the first time he placed his right hand in the middle of my back. He introduced me to other Alexander Technique students whose work overlapped with mine and he taught me to think and write precisely about the Technique. I owe him a great debt.

Elizabeth Langford

In the early days of the training course at Lansdowne Road, our numbers were small enough for general conversation.

I remember Kri Ackers raging about the discouragement felt by a friend of hers on being told by the medics that there was nothing to be done for her condition and she "would have to learn to live with it". Walter continued working with me as he murmured, "Oh yes, Christine, they do say that. Quite right, that's what they say. Yes, indeed they do. That's right, they do, they do indeed". After a pause for inhibition, presumably he decided that this was an occasion for justifiable wrath. He let go of me, took the time to come out of monkey and reach his full height, and in a splendidly produced voice that could have filled Covent Garden Opera House, he shouted the one word: "BASTARDS!"

Monique Vanormelingen

Walter's lectures during the 2004 International AT Congress at Oxford were remarkable not only for their content, but for the way he surmounted the acoustic problems that all speakers encountered. He listened to the echoing acoustic and allowed for it in the speed of his delivery. If someone coughed or a chair squeaked – masking an important word – Walter simply picked up the missing word in the next sentence. On one occasion, the microphones broke down – no problem, one could still hear what Walter was saying, so excellent was his voice production. Clearly, his underlying concern was that everyone should be able to follow the thread of his argument.

His performance was a superb lesson in awareness and application of the Technique. With or without amplification, Walter in his ninetieth year was the only speaker I could be certain of hearing properly in those difficult conditions.

Jordi Cardoner

Va ser al principi de la nostra formació, l'any 2004. La Nica ens va suggerir d'anar a Londres. Ens va dir que el Walter es feia gran seria bo que el conguessim. No sé com però vam anar-hi.

El Walter em va mirar, en vafer un gest convidant-me a un torn. En vaig posar nerviós. Recordo la seva mà a la esquenaa, potser encara la sento ara. Recordo elseu somriure i la seva permesa. Vaig estar-hi dos dies més. I el Walter va seguir donant-nos torns a tots.

Va ser emotiu, estar amb la Rosa I la Nica, les nostres professors formades ja fa temps per eli. Va ser uns dies exitants, cordials, plens d'humor i inolvidables.

Translation from the Catalan:
It was the start of our training course, 2004. Nica suggested we should go to London. She told us that Walter was somebody we really must know. I don't quite know how, but somehow we got there.

Walter looked at me, and made a gesture inviting me to have a turn. I was getting nervous. I remember his hand on my back; I think I still feel it now. I remember his smile and his way of helping one to be oneself. For two more days, Walter continued giving turns to all of us.

It was moving for us to be there together with Rosa and Nica, our teachers whom he had trained in the past. Those days were exciting, friendly, full of humour, simply unforgettable.

Silvia Solaesa

Es senillo; llegas y respiras el peso de la historia. Notas la presencia de Walter aunque en ese momento no esté alli. Percibes que cada uno delos que sí están siguen un estímulo similar.

Cuando Walter te pone la manos, cuando reibes un turno simplemente es más fácil.

Translation from the Spanish:
It's simple; you arrive and you breathe the weight of history. You notice Walter's presence even in the moments when he is not there. You perceive that each of the others who are present feels a similar stimulus. When Walter puts a hand on you, when you receive a turn from him, it simply makes things easier.

Tanja Haupt

Fast die gesamte Schule, L'Estudi, aus Barcelona, machte sich im Februar 2005 auf den Weg nach London, um das Constructive Teaching Centre zu besuchen.

Unsere spanische Bande wurde von allen sehr herzlich aufgenommen, und dafür an diese Stelle nochmals vielen Dank.

Walter Carrington bewegte uns mit "einem Finger", seinem vereinnehmenden Lachen und Lächeln, seinen alles überblickenden Augen, siener Präsenz und seinen ruhenden Händen. Eine wundervolle, eindrucksvolle Erfahrung, die fest in mein Herz und meinen welteren Weg eingebunden ist.

Translation from the German:
Nearly the entire school (L'Estudi, from Barcelona) travelled to London in February 2005, to visit the Constructive Teaching Centre.

Our Spanish group was welcomed very cordially, and for this, again, many thanks.

Walter Carrington moved us with one finger, with his captivating laughter and smile, with his all-seeing eyes, his presence and his calm hands. A wonderful, impressive experience, which is firmly entwined in my heart and my future.

Dominique Jacques

Here is a story about Walter that I have been telling my students again and again over the years:

It is about Walter's great power of inhibition and compassion.

We were in the training room at Lansdowne Road. It was a regular morning; Walter and other teachers were giving us turns. The room was full of directing students and teachers. Karen Wentworth was there as a student every day with her little boy Forrest.

At some point Forrest, who had climbed a chair, fell and started to cry. When Walter saw Forrest crying, he did not react at all. He kept working while he was looking at Forrest with a benevolent big smile. What struck me was that he did not attempt to help Forrest nor did he pretend to go and help. The expression on his face did not show any sign of "what an unfortunate thing just happened, how sad, poor Forrest, I wish I could help". Instead his face manifested that all was well, a child falling, a child crying was just part of life and there was no need to react or feel sorry.

Karen crossed the room to go with Forrest and life in Lansdowne Road continued.

Now sometimes when I witness an unfortunate event and I am too far away or not the appropriate person to help directly, I find myself not reacting, but with compassion, and I think of Walter.

Barbara Harrington

I qualified as an Alexander teacher from Walter's course in July 1981. Walter gave me my life: he made FM's principles accessible to me, and he offered me a personal way forward.

Teaching the Alexander Technique has also provided my sole means of income and support, and I feel so fortunate to have such fascinating and absorbing work.

Without the generosity of Walter and Dilys, none of this would have been possible. They helped me financially, by giving me a job as Walter's secretary. I imagine I was the worst secretary ever, but he was always patient with me! There were so many other ways in which both Walter and Dilys extended generosity towards me and I shall always be grateful to both of them.

Walter's wisdom and presence have walked with me and inspired me, and will continue to do so throughout my life.

Memories of
WALTER from Peri Aston
large gentle warm hands working
their magic
Kind smile and considerate attention.
Absolute refusal to be pinned
Down!
Thoughtful and fair
totally his own person
full of spirit and integrity
and
a Master of his craft

Monika Straakholder

I feel deeply grateful to Walter and Dilys. Some way through my training with them (1986–89) Dilys had the splendid idea that I could do the cleaning of the teaching rooms in exchange for living upstairs. Absorbing that privileged atmosphere of trust, security and reliability, I was as happy as can be.

One afternoon, I had a strong spell of dizziness. Walter heard about it and came to my room to give me a turn. I so much appreciated this generous and helpful gesture. I shall keep Walter in my heart – a personality of great integrity, knowledge, experience, and sense of humour.

Elizabeth Langford

Walter's humour might sometimes surprise us, but it always had a bearing on our work. Once – in those days there was plenty of room to spare – Edward Gellatly, one of the assistant teachers, was in a deep monkey, his back towards the table where I was lying. As Walter swung me off the table, he deliberately used my feet to give Edward an unexpected biff in the backside. Edward jumped. The class laughed. Walter said demurely, "Thank you, Betty, I thought I could rely on you to inhibit."

Another time, Kri Ackers asked, "What should I do if a pupil stiffens so much that I can't support them without hurting myself?" The answer was unhesitating. "Drop them, Christine!"

As we laughed, Walter went on to explain that the pupil is "a going concern". He came for a lesson under his own steam, and will leave without our help. We should not give him the idea we are taking responsibility for everything he does.

Walter brought the same truth home to me in my early days on the training course, when my legs used to shake a lot on the table. (I had managed to get confused as to the difference between *doing* and *directing*; and probably had some lurking idea that *not doing* meant *relaxing*.) It was all very baffling for all of us, until Walter said to me, "For heaven's sake, Betty, they are your legs". Then it became simple: they were my legs and I was in charge of them.

Successive generations of students were told that one of the Carrington sons, then a schoolboy, had remarked, "You know, Dad, your work is dead menial".

Walter took delight in relating this, and his comment was typical. "Well, of course he was right, if you define 'menial' as doing for people what they ought to do for themselves." It didn't perturb him - nor did it deter him from using his astonishing skill in the service of making learning as easy as possible for us.

That skill was so great that it was often impossible to understand. But a student heard to murmur, "Magic!" was told roundly, "It isn't. That is exactly what is NOT. It is systematized common sense".

David Gorman

Walter Carrington. What can I say?

I suppose the first thing is that those of us who trained with him and worked with him all knew him as "Walter", and spoke to him as "Walter". Not "Mr Carrington", not "Sir", just – plain old Walter. That's not to say that there wasn't respect there. I daresay there was more respect for the man, not just because of his obvious knowledge and skill, but also because of his humility and sheer approachableness, than any outward forms of respect could ever have achieved.

When I first heard that Walter had died, I thought, "But he was so young, how could he die?" He wasn't, of course. He was 90, after all. But it was a huge surprise to hear that he had passed away. Of course, the Walter I expected to go on forever was not the flesh and blood man of four score and ten years, but the one whose influence continues to live.

Walter was a master of the art of indirect teaching. I remember one day when he was giving me a turn in the big room of the training course, and he said, "You know, David, I was thinking the other day about breathing". And he proceeded to talk about breathing and function in a way that hit home to me and shed light on my own breathing problems. I not only understood something about breathing I had known before, but my breathing was changed.

It was when I saw him doing similar things with others that I realized Walter had not just *happened* to be "thinking about breathing". He was purposely saying something personal, of a particular relevance to me, but couching it in a general way so I could take it in and think about it in a way that didn't get me focusing inwards or becoming self-conscious. Of course, it was all the more relevant to me and real because his hands were also showing me just what his words meant, but he would never have pointed that out.

Walter was always willing to look at new ideas and evidence. There was no question from us that he wouldn't take seriously. He kept up with the recent scientific research and its implications for the Alexander work, and he encouraged us all to think and pursue the truth of things.

If anyone deserves to be remembered - with boundless respect - as a person and as a teacher, it is Walter.

Tommy Thompson

One remarkable memory I have of Walter - apart from the occasional lessons when I was in London, or his surprising initiative in writing to me to compliment me on an article I'd written, or his genuine concern about the welfare of my family - was of eating in a restaurant in London. Walter was sitting beside me, with Dilys opposite, next to David Gorman.

We were all engaged in conversation when I suddenly became aware of Walter's palpable presence alongside me; it was enormous, his voice resonated from this fullness of being. Of course it was not the first time I had been near him, but in this simple, social context, I was experiencing his proximity quite differently. It seems I had a sudden sense of his lifelong commitment to high-minded principles that were deeply embodied in his own sense of self.

Elizabeth Langford

I doubt if Walter ever stopped integrating the Technique into his daily life.

I remember when some of us were in the pub with him after a long day's work in hot weather. Walter remarked contentedly on yet another reason for freeing the neck and lengthening: you could feel and enjoy the beer going down for longer.

Yvonne Becker

I qualified with Walter and Dilys in July 1983.

I remember one very special lesson:

After lunch Walter demonstrated squatting to the class. Later that afternoon he gave me my turn. I mentioned that I could not squat. Walter continued working on me but without my knowing he quietly removed the chair. He held me at the back of my neck and took me down into the squat and I instantly bobbed up like a cork in the water back into the standing position. It happened so quickly and was such an amazing experience of really being free and moving with direction.

I had squatted!

Walter was such an excellent teacher. He knew how to impart knowledge. He never made anybody feel stupid or inferior.

He was so very helpful to me. When I first started teaching (before e-mails) I used to write to him to ask advice about pupils and their problems. He always found time to reply promptly and in a most helpful way.

In one of his letters, he wrote:

"The Alexander Technique teaches directly the correct use of the self. In other words, it guides one towards the state of freedom and balance of body and mind that is the basis of effective performance in all activities."

With his permission I have often quoted this passage.

He truly lived his philosophy and I admired his compassionate attitude and his understanding nature. I always felt understood and supported. He never criticized and always approached problems from a positive angle. He was so non-judgemental and for that I will always be thankful, as that was such a wonderful role model for me and I try to remember that every day also in my daily life.

I do not think we always knew just how great his influence was on all who knew him and were taught by him. What a privilege to have known such a spirit!

Meredith Page

Walter's unfailing support did not inflate our pride – but fired our courage and confidence. When I mentioned to him with great trepidation that I was rather worried just before I was to give my very first Alexander lesson, he said softly, with a conspiratorial grin, "Just remember, you know a jolly sight more about it than the punter does!"

Rose Bronec

Back in 1982, as a new teacher with only two years of teaching, I wrote to Walter and asked if I could visit for a term, not as a teacher but as a trainee. He was kind and said "yes". I had never been to England. It was a wonderful term in many ways. The private lessons with Walter were the cream at the top.

I'll never forget the lesson when Walter talked about the innate fear of falling as it related to myself as a teacher. Since my lack of confidence and shy tendencies would oftentimes leave me feeling intimidated by my students, Walter assured me that we are all afraid of falling. Therefore, as an Alexander teacher, I had something to offer to anyone. I could help them with that most basic fear, a fear that we all share.

His advice allowed me to see the student as human, minus the superficial habits, the bravado, the excuses. Ever after, when I began to "feel" intimidated by a student, I was able to find my "fear of falling" touchstone. It gave me a place to begin. It allowed me to be "in process". For this, I am grateful. Thank you, Walter.

Ces deux souvenirs sont toujours présents lorsque je pense à Walter.

Le premier souvenir c'est le contact de sa grande main solide dans mon dos, lors des leçons individuelles. Elle me semblait énorme et sécurisante et je pouvais lâcher prise et laisser mon dos s'ouvrir à plus d'espace en longueur et en largeur. Quelle merveilleuse expérience! MERCI WALTER!

L'autre souvenir se situe à la reprise des cours après les vacances d'été en 1983 à Lansdowne Road. C'est un grand jour car je commence le "teaching term". Dans la grande salle, Walter donne des mini leçons aux élèves et aux jeunes gradués comme moi. Lorsque mon tour arrive, je ne manque pas de faire part à Walter de mes inquiétudes d'enseigner. Walter écoute sans rien dire et maintient le cap sur le "travail". N'ayant aucune réaction de la part de Walter, je réalise soudainement qu'il n'y a pas de quoi s'attarder sur des scénarios reliés à des vieux schèmes. La leçon une fois terminée, je me dirige sans hésitation vers ma première expérience officielle d'enseignante sans être incommodée par la suite. En restant attentive aux "moyens" les fantômes disparaissent.

Sans qu'aucun mot ait été dit, les directions renouvelées de Walter ont fait tomber mes interférences. Pendant trois ans, j'ai reçu et intégré un enseignement, le temps était venu de le mettre à profit.

Même si cela fait bien des années que je ne l'ai pas revu le lien reste, et ma gratitude est immense. Sa voix, surtout son rire restent au présent.

Translation of the French:
These two memories are always present when I think of Walter.

The first is the touch of his big solid hand on my back during individual lessons. That hand seemed to me enormous and reassuring: I could let go and allow my back to open out into more space, both in length and width. What a marvellous experience!
THANK YOU WALTER!

The other memory is of the beginning of term at Lansdowne Road after the summer holidays in 1983. This is a big day for me, the start of my "teaching term". In the big students' room, Walter is giving short lessons to students and to new graduates like me. When it is my turn, I share with him my worries about teaching. Walter listens in silence, remaining focussed on the work. Getting no reaction from him, I suddenly realize that there is no need to linger on scenarios related to old patterns of thinking. Once my lesson is over, I move without hesitation towards my first official experience as a teacher, quite unconcerned. I remain attentive to the "means" and my anxiety disappears.

Without a word, Walter's directions, renewed in me, have broken through my interference. For three years I have received and integrated his teaching; now it is time to put it to work.

Even though it is years since I saw him, the link remains and my gratitude is immense. His voice, his laugh above all, are always present.

Hege Falch Irgens

Walter was and still is the greatest man I ever met in my life. What he has been teaching me, is still growing and changing.

I came to Lansdowne Road in 1983 to become an Alexander Teacher. I was 23 years old, shy and lost in the big world. Walter and Dilys kindly let me stay in their house upstairs. Part of the deal was to clean the classrooms and iron Walter's shirts. The ironing took me hours and the shirts were still looking as if they had not been ironed at all. A teacher downstairs came to the rescue and did all 5 shirts in 15 minutes. The second load of shirts for ironing never turned up!

There are two sayings by Walter that have stayed close to me for 22 years and have made a deep impact in me, both in a teaching way and as a road-sign, pointing the direction on the path of life.

The first thing is when I nervously asked Walter for advice when I was going to give my first lesson. He kindly and calmingly said: "Get your directions going, go into monkey and put your hands on". So I did and still do.

The second thing that I remember him saying and still stick to was the words that woke me up at one of his lectures: "Keep your aim and frame it in your mind".

Jeanne Day

After giving a lesson at Lansdowne Road in 1964 and feeling keenly my lack of experience, I met Walter in the hallway.

"Walter," I said, "I don't think I really know what I'm doing!"

He replied, "Neither do I, Jeanne, neither do I! Never mind – just make soothing noises and take the money!"

I went away smiling.

I have carried this with me all through my teaching life, and often repeated it to trainees who are getting nervous at the prospect of qualifying.

Walter never stopped reminding us that all knowledge is incomplete, but that that fact need not deter us from making proper use of what we do know. Experience only comes with experience. (Ed.)

John Nicholls

When I first joined the training course at Lansdowne Road in 1973, I was struck by Walter's calm and kind demeanor and the sense that here was a man with great depth of knowledge of this mysterious subject, the Alexander Technique. I was in such a personal state of turmoil at the time that I was not even really aware of his mastery as a teacher of the Technique, but the hours of training each day were an oasis of order and tranquillity in my otherwise disordered life.

As I went on through the training, and then worked as an assistant teacher for many years at Lansdowne Road, I came to value and appreciate more and more, along with his immense skill in teaching, those personal qualities. So much so that when a visitor once said to me at the end of a day in class "I'd love to know what lies behind that mask of benevolence," I could only answer: "I've been around him five days a week for more than ten years and I really believe that behind that mask of benevolence there lies a truly benevolent man".

That word benevolence inevitably comes up when anyone who knew Walter talks about him. It was used in the caption under his photo in the obituary in *The Times*. Benevolence is an attitude of positive goodwill towards everyone. It seemed to go with an attitude of self acceptance and contentedness in his own life. I once asked him if that came from a lifetime of putting the Alexander Technique into practice. He laughed heartily, and then replied: "Well, I don't know what else it could be!"

At times, standing near him as he gave turns on the training course, this quality was almost palpable, radiating from him like a personal energy field.

One day while giving me a turn in class, Walter repeated a saying he'd heard somewhere: "They say all wise men are of the same religion. But what that religion is, no wise man will ever tell you." In religious traditions that wonderful quality of acceptance and benevolence that Walter conveyed to everyone might be called impersonal love. I know that after abandoning his early interest in joining the Jesuits, Walter did not espouse any religion. But under the purview of any religion, or none, impersonal love is a remarkably high aspiration and attainment.

Of course, this quality also enhanced the mastery of his hands. Through the repeated experience of his hands I came to understand that in order to change you must be able to accept how you are as your starting point, and feeling that you are accepted is a great aid in that process. Often in the two-minute turns that he would give all of us, teachers and students alike, each afternoon, I would feel as his hands first came on to me an immediate amplification of my own sense of myself. My deep underlying pattern of use would come more clearly into my consciousness. And yet there was also an underlying feeling tone of "It's OK to be who you are." Or, as I often heard Walter say: "If you've become aware that you're stiffening and pulling yourself down, the first thing to do is say to yourself, well, that's the way it is." Of course, paradoxically, it then became possible to consider that changing would be all right too. In this way Walter conveyed to us that acceptance and self-acceptance are crucial to the practice of inhibition and direction.

I have at times heard Walter say that late on in FM's life, he realized that people took in far less of the content of what he said than the manner in which he said it, plus, of course, the quality of the experience they were getting from his hands. Sometime in my second year of training, I had a vivid experience of how that might have been. As Walter gave me a turn one day in class, working with his hands on my lower ribs, my breathing suddenly became uncontrollable shudders, and deeply held distress burst out of me in the form of both sobbing and hysterical laughter. Incipient panic was dispelled by Walter's powerful yet gentle hands supporting me, and the totally accepting and reassuring way in which he repeatedly said, "It's the diaphragm, John. It's just the diaphragm". Looking back I think he could have said absolutely anything at that moment. What counted was not the words, but the message of quietly benign acceptance conveyed from every aspect of his being.

Some years later, when I was teaching at Lansdowne Road and was consulted by the producer of a planned British TV documentary on the Alexander Technique, I took him to interview Walter expecting he would feature Walter in the film. The producer later decided to feature another first generation teacher instead, and I conveyed this news somewhat apologetically to Walter. His response was very characteristic: "Good Heavens, don't worry about that. You know I'm not in the least bit concerned about such things." And he wasn't. Part of what made him a wonderful teacher was that he really, really didn't concern himself with being seen as a wonderful teacher. You knew he was working to help you, not to impress you. This was also apparent in his generosity in answering questions. Some master teachers in many fields succumb a little to the temptation to hold back something, to create an aura of mystique that enhances their personal power. I never saw a trace of that in Walter. The more able you became to articulate precise questions about teaching, the more fully and freely he would share his knowledge and experience.

In 1988 when I was living and working in Melbourne, Australia, Walter and Dilys came to visit. We arranged for Walter to deliver a public lecture on F.M. Alexander at Melbourne University. Since Melbourne was the birthplace of the Alexander Technique, an audience of several hundred people turned out to hear about this work that had originated in their city. Walter delivered a fine talk, portraying both something of the character of FM and the nature of his discoveries. We teachers were sitting there feeling very pleased with how the event was going, when someone got up from the audience and began fervently speaking about their own experience of a visit to Lansdowne Road in London, and their own views about the Alexander Technique. These views were somewhat eccentric, not really what those of us teaching in Melbourne would have wanted a large gathering of our fellow citizens to hear as a first impression of the Technique. We were embarrassed. We wanted this person to sit down and stop talking.

Walter sat on the platform listening with that same aura of calm acceptance and goodwill that he brought to all of his life. It appeared he did not allow a molecule of discomfort or disapproval to enter his being. When the intervening speaker had finished he thanked her with genuine graciousness for her contribution. A last question was allowed from the audience, and Walter was challenged to demonstrate rising from a chair with good use. He beamed at the questioner as he sat and talked about how awkward such a question might be, and how it made him aware of all the possibilities of being nervous with so many people watching him being put to the test in this very public arena. And then he rose lightly and easily to his feet with an open-faced, open-hearted smile.

The Dean of Melbourne University, who had never met Walter before this evening, closed proceedings by telling the audience that tonight we had enjoyed the privilege of having the life and work of one great man described to us by another great man.

Thank you, Walter.

Micheline Charron

Walter had a great sense both of self and of selflessness while demonstrating strength and stability in his teaching. He had clarity in thinking which helped us, as I observed in myself and others around me, to find our way in using our own thinking abilities. He was very generous. He also taught us to remain positive with compassion and lots of humor and laughter. He was fully committed to the advancement of the Technique, to the pedagogy of learning and to opening possibilities for people.

It was shocking news that Walter has left us. It has been hard work of letting go of the idea that he was eternal. Not another habit to let go of, my God!

I console myself with the thought that the quality of his presence is eternal, just as his teaching will continue to influence eternity.

Michael J. Gelb

Walter was *extraordinary* because he was the gently consistent stalwart of a world in which unconditional kindness, commitment to continuous learning and intelligent consideration of the Use of the Self were *ordinary*.

Ilana Machover

In my last lesson with him last year, I asked Walter something relating to FM. And he answered, "You know, FM was also a very practical man". And he told me the following story to illustrate FM's practicality:

"One day I entered his teaching room and tried to draw the curtains. I had some difficulty with this, and FM said to me: 'Walter, there is no need to move the curtain by pulling it down; try to take it upwards, and then move it'. And of course he was right!"

I was so perplexed that I came back home and immediately tried to follow these instructions. Bingo! So simple.

Jacob Heringman

I'm sorry to say I only had one lesson with Walter, and it was in my very first term on Karen Wentworth's training course. That lesson stayed with me, and I often think about it. Here are some notes written immediately after the lesson.

Walter asked me what I do - was very interested to hear it's lute - said years ago he taught a lutenist.

He worked purely in chair (and out of chair but never for long). Sure and confident and knowing hands, strong and inquiring, but never forceful.

Walter: You've clearly already solved several problems for yourself.
Me: But on the lute of course it's taking a lot longer.
Walter: As you change and develop in this work, you'll increasingly find what you need to change in your lute-playing, and you'll be able to reason out for yourself how to adjust your technique on the instrument.

Walter: Technique on an instrument is one thing, but beyond technique, way beyond technique, is communication with the people you're playing for. If you are free and going up, it will be communicated to the audience. If you're afraid, pulling down, thinking "this is hard", the audience will receive this message as well.

Some of the other points Walter discussed:

When we're having lessons we have to keep remembering our directions, of course.

"But I'm afraid", he said, "that you and I have to keep on remembering them for the rest of our lives. Pity it doesn't just happen automatically."

"For instance," he went on to say, "we keep the neck free and the head going forward and up, etc., when we're standing or sitting. But when we're about to go from one to the other, we tend to tighten in the legs or hips, and our attention shifts to those points and away from the head-neck-back. What's got to happen, of course, is that we must include the thought of not tightening the hips and legs in preparation for sitting or standing, along with the head-neck-back directions."

He said that in four-footed creatures, the proper angle of back legs to spine creates the stretch of the spine towards the pelvis (I paraphrase, I hope, correctly.) And of course the animal wants to move forward so the head, naturally enough, leads. It's very clear in animals. We must remember to keep thinking the two-way stretch in ourselves, and leave the pelvis on the chair when we get up. If you're going to stretch a piece of string, you don't just pull on one end.

All vertebrates, from snakes to humans, have a mechanism to mobilize the spine for action. This involves creating freedom or space between all of the vertebrae. "You don't see a lot of snakes with slipped discs!"

Nick Chapman

Walter always said that learning the Alexander Technique enhanced your learning ability. When I started training, I decided to test this theory by learning the flute, an instrument that I had always wanted to play. Every day at break time I would sneak into one of the teaching rooms at Lansdowne Road and start to teach myself the flute. By the end of my training I had had several different flute teachers. One day when I was about to have a private lesson with Walter, he told me to bring my flute.

I had a great sense that this was a rare treat, though I had no idea of how profound an influence he would really have on my flute playing and on my approach to learning anything from that time onwards. It was strange to find that Walter, who didn't play the flute, could help me play so much better than I had ever done before.

Elizabeth Langford

During the second year of my training, Anthony Green and I gave an important recital. To my great joy, Walter and Dilys not only came to the concert, but gave me a turn in the artists' room beforehand and in the interval. I walked on to the platform feeling marvellous and ready to do my best.

Like so many of his pupils, I can say that Walter was always there with encouragement when I most needed it. Several times it was by taking an interest in something I had written. I shall always treasure the note he sent when my energy was at its lowest after a cancer operation: he said he had been taking some of my former students and they were a credit to me. Nothing could have helped me more than that word of approval.

Walter was always very encouraging in my efforts with regard to the theatre. For him it was axiomatic to encourage potential. He understood in practice what it means to encourage someone to engage in something within their aspirations, but perhaps a little outside their daring.

In 1982 he insisted on a demonstration in class of some clown work I had experienced in a course given by the great clown teacher Philippe Gaulier. I was a bit reluctant and nervous, but wanted to do it, deep down. I needed a push. After two or three weeks of waiting for me he asked me one day when I was going to do it - in that tone of voice that meant "when are you going to make up your mind to do it?" "Next Tuesday" I gulped. Why it was Tuesday I don't remember.

In clown work it takes months and years to evolve a repertoire of things that your clown can do to make the audience laugh. So I only had a few minutes' worth. The day came and Walter agreed to introduce a "special, unexpected guest who has just returned from California who is going to talk about breathing". I made my entrance, got an immediate laugh and, as I had been taught, went out again, because since they had enjoyed that entrance so much, I thought I would do another one. This placed Walter on the spot ("*dans la merde*" as we had learned to say in the Gaulier course) since he was on his own again. But he managed to carry on chatting and introducing despite my unexpected disappearance. Not bad, I thought, to say the least, for someone without experience, as far as I know, in theatrical improvisation. I did another entrance and then stayed in. He let me stay and chat to the students about it afterwards for much more than the allotted lecture time. That memory will certainly remain.

In 1989 he came to Denmark to a special conference that Chris Stevens arranged. The conference was to include a version of the "Midsummer Night's Dream" by William Shakespeare in which I had directed the students at Chris's training course. One learns in theatre that the final character to appear, the one who completes and who finally reveals the performance, is the audience. I would swear Walter held the production together by himself, sitting in the audience.

Much has been said, especially by a member of Walter's aircrew during the war, of Walter's ability to transmit calmness and confidence to those around him. Well, there it was. The actors noticed it too. Our nervousness seemed to diminish, and my doubts as to how it would turn out ceased to be a worry.

Walter recalled and talked about the performance several times in the months afterwards. I was so glad that there seemed to be something about it that struck a chord with him.

Last year, he encouraged me to write a pamphlet setting out my understanding of the connections between Alexander lessons and theatre skills. I find it a funny business, writing about something one cares about but which one has worked out basically for oneself, not necessarily for others. At the same time, perhaps these are things one really should be putting on paper. In a way, it was written on demand from Walter - another push for which I was very grateful.

On this occasion I learned another lesson: that one can do something out of one's ordinary when asked by someone for whom one has infinite admiration and trust.

During a short turn on the course, Walter started working on my shoulders which were very tight and he said I had to learn to "shimmy" if I was to get them to free up. Good advice to a woman who loved to dance.

He had guessed that I was into ballet because I had the body of a dancer with very strong legs and my lower back pulled in, and indeed I had studied ballet for a few years but then abandoned the idea of training.

Hanna Sypianska

"With happy memories of our riding on Wednesday afternoons", Walter Carrington wrote on a picture I took with me back to Poland.

When I think about Walter, what strikes me most is not his knowledge, brightness, eloquence, unbelievable patience and stamina, not even his sense of humour.

I remember the feeling I had in his presence, of space, lightness and freedom both in my mind and body.

His accepting curiosity allowed things to happen in their own way, so easily.

As an uncertain stranger, I was lucky enough to meet a true English gentleman, so I learnt what that could mean.

Thank you, Walter.

You taught me how to fly.

Judith Youett Muir

I was privileged to meet Walter Carrington over 28 years ago after I moved to London and ended up living just twenty minutes walk from Lansdowne Rd. Of course in those days I had no idea at all about either his existence, or that of the Constructive Teaching Centre. I was looking for an Alexander Teacher, after a year of no lessons, and finally got around to making a telephone call on the recommendation of a friend of mine.

This continuation of lessons led me to hear a lot about what a great teacher Walter Carrington was and how difficult it was to get a lesson from him, as he was booked up three months in advance. Believing with all the assurance of youth that no one could be THAT good, I managed to book my lesson for some distant time in the future.

The lesson itself seemed very unremarkable and I thought that Walter droned on about this and that. Nothing stuck out in particular, and I went my merry way home. As usual I threw myself onto my sofa in my usual way and immediately leapt back up as everything in my body rebelled at how I had moved. I remember apologizing to myself. Then I sat down with much more thought to the means whereby and decided that this guy was amazing.

Dilys Carrington decided that she wanted me to be the next secretary, so I was paid to train as a teacher of the Alexander Technique. One of my jobs was to book all Walter's appointments, a term at a time. Since most of his pupils were regulars who had come for years, there were very few free spaces. One time I managed somehow to give away a regular pupil's lesson time and hoped that Walter would go along with this. Little did I know!

Having got up the nerve to confess my error to Walter, (secretly hoping that I would not have to make a phone call to correct my mistake, and worried that I would get yelled at) I was on the receiving end of a big beaming smile and the words, "Well, you will just have to correct it".

Over the years at Lansdowne Rd, at the desk and on the training course, I saw Walter work with many different, often difficult people in a wide variety of settings, and was always impressed with his unfailing patience and willingness to teach and help. He lived what he understood the Alexander Technique to be, and never lost his faith in the possibility that this work could help everyone. He was a remarkable man who lived a long and productive life. It was a privilege to have seen and worked with him in so many different ways.

Mary McGovern

Two memories immediately come to mind when I think about Walter.

I asked him one day how he always seemed to manage to be cheerful. In three years on his training course I had never seen him cross or irritated. His reply was, "Practise, my dear, practise!" I have taken it as a lesson for life. A mental attitude can be practised and perfected just as well as a physical one.

"That's just the way it is" was a phrase Walter often used. No matter how stressed or unhappy one was when one arrived for a lesson, he would say, "Well, that's just the way it is", often followed by, "Now let's see where we can go from here".

We all have our ups and downs in daily life, some days being more of a challenge than others. I found his acceptance of the situation presented by the pupil as a starting point for lengthening and widening very comforting and reassuring. There was no blame or criticism, just a complete acceptance of one's present physical and emotional situation.

Throughout my training with Walter and Dilys, I had to keep working as a musician in order to pay the mortgage, etc. I often came home very late from a show (and the inevitable pub afterwards!) and some days in the class I felt pretty sluggish, to say the least.

On one particular occasion, I must have been pretty tired and unable to generate any semblance of "up". Walter came around as usual in the afternoon session and gave us all a turn. When my number came up, I was having a nice pull down in a quiet corner and preparing for an afternoon snooze.

Something happened to me in the few minutes that followed that can not very easily be described in words. All I vividly remember is hearing Dilys from the other side of the room saying, rather sternly, "Shake him like a dog, Walter!" And, oh boy, he did! But in such an extraordinary way that my body somehow sprang back into life, and I was even able to go off and work on someone else.

Walter's skill was really quite unique, and I think all of us who were lucky enough to have trained with him and Dilys will treasure such moments for the rest of our lives.

Marta Barón

In my training with Walter and Dilys Carrington I used to have more or less monthly lessons with Walter in my last year. In the first lesson, despite the fact that I had already had turns from him, I was a bit worried. He was the master, the person many people spoke of with utter admiration and almost reverence. After that lesson, I knew everything would be all right. He was a down-to-earth, generous man.

Every lesson with Walter was an adventure. I never knew what would happen and was absolutely delighted at the prospect of discovering something, having a laugh with him, or simply listening to some interesting story that he was in the mood to tell me.

This particular lesson was just another one. Walter was not to be disturbed while teaching. However – making use of the flexible nature of the work – if something happened, he would not be surprised or uncomfortable if someone came into the room and asked something.

I could hear Ruth talking on the phone and then a knock on the door. She popped her head round and said that he had to pick up the phone and sort something out with the bank.

Now I could hear his voice, at first just calm and asking what was the matter, saying, "Yes, Walter Carrington speaking". Then his tone rose a little bit and he started to answer very curtly, showing that he was not happy at all. At some point he said, "Yes, you are wasting my time" with a tone unknown to me in Walter. Then immediately, "Yes, I am absolutely furious" and he put the phone down in such a way that I could distinctly hear the crash with the desk.

One minute, maybe two. And then he came back and put his hand on my neck saying, "I'm sorry my dear, they don't do their job properly and they have to disturb everyone."

I could feel his hand on my neck, the tone of it completely different to the hand that had left it two minutes ago. It was as if he knew by experience that the difference demanded some adjustment, so he left his hand there for quite some time before doing anything else. I could feel he was working on himself, stopping, directing, undoing all the anger and reversing it into some constructive train of thought.

After some time he was back to normal, the disturbance not disturbing the lesson any more. I remember thinking: "psychophysical unity at work".

Jeanne Day

Kri Ackers and I knew each other quite well at Lansdowne Rd. I told her recently of an incident I remembered which she insists is worth repeating. When Kri had been a short time on the course I asked, in a rather superior tone, "Walter, why is that girl lying about on the floor all the time as if she were dead?" I don't remember his exact words but he rounded on me in hot defence of Kri, leaving me in no uncertain terms squashed flat!

Noel Kingsley

I have found writing about Walter the most difficult thing ever. I lived in his house for over 13 years and have so many memories. Everything I think of writing seems lacking and incomplete. When remembering Walter, I'm flooded with images: his hands, his gentle and lively humour, his patience, love and generosity; also his more private side, his home life. I find myself unable to express these memories satisfactorily. He is always with me and I loved him dearly.

Meredith Page

During World War II, Walter served in the Royal Air Force as a Pathfinder pilot. (Ed.)

By coincidence, I happen now to live in the same city as Mervyn Bradford, Walter's wartime navigator. Some years ago Walter telephoned me to ask if I would give some Alexander lessons to his friend, "Brick", as Mervyn was dubbed by his RAF colleagues. Brick is still around and very sprightly at eighty-three. He has told me about their hazardous forays over enemy territory. He describes with a mixture of deep affection and awe how "Carrie" (Walter) always had the most extraordinary effect on his crew – a calming, coherent field of consciousness seemed to emanate from him and fill the entire aircraft with peace. Brick says that no matter what the danger, everyone remained focussed, level-headed and quiet because they had such faith in Walter's impeccable leadership.

Brick has often told me of the moment late in 1944 when an enemy fighter fired two rockets into their left wing and fuel tanks. Their bomber instantly erupted into flames and went into a corkscrew dive. Brick says that most pilots would have put the plane on auto-pilot and made a parachute jump, leaving the crew to do likewise. Had Walter done that, they would all have been killed. Walter remained in the cockpit, struggling to stabilise the aircraft until all his crew had jumped safely.

Only Walter himself was badly injured. When he finally jumped, he probably got pulled into the slipstream by the heat and turbulence, or else the safety harness of his parachute was momentarily caught on something. He landed quite close to the plane as it crashed.

The enemy would usually approach downed aircraft very promptly, but instead of escaping, the crew all ran to Walter to try to help him. He was lying on his back in a crumpled twist, one of his eyes had come out of its socket and was dangling on his cheekbone, his jaw was broken, and he had a terrible gash in his head. At this point Hungarian soldiers and police arrived and captured them. One of the enemy looked down at Walter and said, "Leave him - he's dead". Whereupon Walter opened his good eye, looked up and said, "Oh no I'm not".

They were carted off to various holding points and Walter was placed under guard in a local farmhouse. He was later rescued by a Jesuit priest who got him to the Russian front where the Russians took admirable care of him and finally flew him back to London. Typically, Walter's first action was to inform the parents of his crew that they were safe.

(Walter knew I am of Russian descent and often told me stories about his time with the Russian officers who were "thoroughly decent chaps".)

This was the origin of the shattered pelvis, which plagued Walter in later life with increasing pain - not that he ever let on. He simply rose above it with his indefatigable humour, quiet determination and a rigorous application of the Alexander Technique.

Walter was too modest to talk much about his wartime experiences, nor did he ever receive any official recognition of his bravery and self-sacrifice - valour that ought to have earned him the highest decoration - not that he would have wanted it. It seems appropriate now, however, not to let this go entirely without a mention.

Leah Landau

About two years ago I had my last private lesson, when I asked Walter about his hip injury and he told me about his experiences as a pilot during the Second World War. I was struck by his stoicism and courage and also the way he recounted his story as if it was rather ordinary. When I reflected on it later I thought of him as a real hero – he lived each day as if it really mattered having faced death and been spared. He said, "I was so glad to be alive". I so admired his dedication and ability to keep on going and giving of his best each day.

In turn, I found myself telling him about a relative of mine escaping from Nazi Germany at the age of fourteen. His usual expression was serious, and I had been glad to see him smiling and laughing after lessons with Walter – who had never felt it necessary to ask about his experiences.

Walter was very subtle: he would work indirectly, and insisted that we did too. It is so tempting in this age of psychotherapy and life-coaching to give advice or draw out the "story" that underlies the psycho-physical habit patterns but Walter always stuck to what FM had taught him. I struggled with this during my training because I do believe in the "talking cure" – but perhaps Walter was right not to try and combine the two disciplines. He always maintained that we had enough to do just to learn to inhibit and direct.

Elizabeth Langford

During one of my first lessons with Walter, I started to tell him briefly about my recent disappointment in a job where everything had gone wrong, including my health. I added, "I am still trying to understand what happened and to face up to it". (At the time, I was seriously interested in psychology - my own and other people's.)

Walter didn't argue with me. He just said, "That may be a very good thing to do, but if I were you I'd put it aside until you are a bit stronger". Put like that, it didn't seem difficult or complicated to practise inhibition.

Ken J. Thompson

One example of Walter's unique style of teaching was how quickly he could assess the needs of a pupil, and provide the right strategy for imparting the Technique.

One day during my training, we had some visitors, friends of one of the students on the course. As Walter made his way around the room giving turns to everyone, he stopped by these people and invited the man to come and stand in front of a chair. Now this guy was completely new to the Alexander Technique, and as Walter put his hand on to his back, the guy turned to him and said slightly aggressively, "What are you doing?"

We who were close by pricked up our ears and tried to watch and listen to see how Walter would deal with this difficult question. As students, of course, we were all thinking how we would try to explain the basic aspects of the Technique to this man, and all the usual things went through our minds: the importance of the head-neck-back relationship, the need for inhibition, etc., etc. But what did Walter do?

Well, he took his hand off, looked the man in the eyes and said, "I'm going to balance you up a bit". We watched in amazement as the guy said agreeably, "Oh, OK then". At that, Walter proceeded to put hands on, take the fellow up, then in and out of the chair. The expression on this guy's face was a treat. You could tell he was going to go away with a positive attitude to the Technique.

Walter had this ability to simplify something that we know is quite difficult to explain to most people, and also to know exactly what will suit each individual, and each situation. He really was expert at it.

Many of us who went through the three years training – and got to know Walter and Dilys so well – realise that we have inherited a direct legacy from F. Matthias Alexander. We hope to stay true to that legacy by endeavouring to follow the basic principles of Alexander's discoveries in all our teaching. We owe it to the future of the work, and to our respect for a great man, friend, and colleague.

Thank you Walter, for influencing our lives.

Frances Marsden

I first met Walter in 1975 at my "interview" at the Constructive Teaching Center. It was all very informal and I was immediately struck by his kindness and consideration. I remember feeling uncomfortable because the sun was shining in my eyes, but Walter put me at ease with, "Is the sun in your eyes, my dear?" When he put a hand on me, there was no sense that he was watching my "Use" or assessing me. Here was a kind person who wanted to welcome me into the work and make me feel at ease.

On the training course, I found him to be as I remembered him from my interview, always open and respectful. You sensed his undivided attention in daily turns with him. He made you feel you were the most important person to him at that moment. As a result, each of us on the training course felt we had a special relationship with him. This was magnified in our private lessons with him. When he closed the door to his teaching room, there was an atmosphere of timelessness inside. Walter, within minutes, skilfully and without judgment, tuned into my nervous system and found the places where I was interfering. Some lessons had an ethereal quality and yet I sensed my connection to the ground.

During the period of the day called "Games", Walter would ask someone to demonstrate the procedure. When it was my turn, my fear reflexes could have been stimulated in front of 35 people. But I always knew that with Walter's hands on me, I'd be able to do the procedure. During our weekly half-hour group with Walter, again his unhurried, reassuring manner encouraged us to feel confident and at ease. He made "hands on" natural and effortless. The most valuable lesson was that we could take our time.

Looking back, I can see that there was a definite structure and content to the course, worked out with great care. You weren't made aware of that, so were free to have your own experience. Walter always began his talk and "Games" at the exact appointed time – you could count on that, but it was never imposed on you. It was all part of an indirect approach which encouraged responsibility from within. There was no pressure to gather information. You could relax and allow it to come to you when you were ready for it, in your own time. I felt valued as an individual for my own way of learning. Walter knew so much, was so erudite, but he never set himself up as an authority. He had a simple, clear purpose – to remain true to Alexander and his principles. In his teaching, he always returned to "the work".

In my third year of training, I went to a STAT meeting with fellow trainees. Walter was challenged at the meeting and stood up to clarify his position. You could see inhibition and direction working in him – you could see his back working. He had such dignity and poise and I felt honored to know someone who so perfectly embodied the work.

The week of his death, I was taking the Refresher Course and invited my friend of training days to come back to Lansdowne Road to visit Dilys. She was moved by the humbleness and simplicity of the school after all these years. That's how I remember Walter – humble and truthful to this wonderful work, with that rare capacity to treat everyone he met with kindness and respect. I'm so grateful for the gifts he gave me as my teacher and I will treasure his memory.

Tasha Miller

I remember vividly my first private lesson with Walter. As the time drew nearer to my meeting him, I could feel my "unduly excited fear reflexes" swelling up in me in their habitual way. I had heard so much about him. His status seemed almost God-like within the Alexander community. I felt very anxious indeed about meeting him and in particular how I should address him. The teachers and students all seemed to call him "Walter" – but would that be presumptuous on my part? Should I call him "Walter" or "Mr. Carrington"? I decided to ask him directly. He smiled in his kind way, seeming a little amused, yet somehow pleased. He said that Walter was his name and that would do just fine, my dear.

I didn't know Walter as closely as some, though I had quite a few lessons with him over a period of years. In each one of those lessons a small step was taken, in a small and beautiful way. Nothing was ever grand or large with Walter and I liked that. The world around us, from childhood to adulthood, is full of exaggerated attitudes. I felt a deep quietening and relief in myself when having a lesson with Walter.

I would have liked to get to know him a little better, though I believe that he was a shy man and at heart a very private person. He had his thoughts, which he kept to himself unless asked to share them.

Frankly, I felt cross with Walter when he did not take a stronger stand against the growing generation of self-promoters and "high achievers". I thought their actions revealed a lack of understanding of Alexander's work – an understanding that was embodied in Walter's every word and deed. They all seemed to me to be after something – power, prestige, raising their profile – something to feed their egos. That was never Walter's style. He was the great gardener, nurturing each seed, allowing it to grow slowly in the way that it needed to, and letting it go just as easily in order that nature could propagate freely.

His final stand spoke about our work with great clarity: above all else this work is about individuals achieving freedom of thought and action in the domain of personal growth and development. The uniqueness of Alexander's technique is not to be appropriated by any one person or body imposing their will on others.

The memory of my first lesson with Walter now seems very pertinent to several currently critical issues, for it implies his own readiness to treat as equals all teachers working with FM's discoveries and technique. It therefore follows that any idea that some can regulate others – or dictate how they should teach – is to some extent misguided. Walter's view was that we should help one another as we can, and celebrate our differences with due respect for each other.

Daniel Pevsner

This is an extract from the tribute at the Memorial Service.(Ed.)

Walter Carrington gave the whole of his being and all of his working life to the cause of the Alexander Technique. He understood its spirit and message and, with the help of his much loved wife and partner, Dilys, gave all his energies to the training of future generations of teachers and to the general promotion of the Technique. Sadly, in recent times he also had to become its protector and its defender. His immediate, urgent legacy to us is best spoken in his own words:

"... these two things - the unity of mind and body, and the attitude towards right and wrong - are the two main features that distinguish our work... It is no good seeing our work like that of anyone else, because it is not. If we are true to our own principles, if we really live the Technique... then there won't be much room for presenting our work as though it was like anything else. To present it as a form of therapy... or to present it as anything other than it is - a psycho-physical process - is to misrepresent and mislead."

Editor's note

The two previous contributions may require a word of explanation, though it would be out of place here to analyse events that are on record elsewhere. Briefly, then:

Walter disliked attempts to "modernize" official descriptions of the Technique. He saw such attempts as misleading, and said, "I do not want the Council to publish or promulgate a description of what we teach that I cannot agree with." He wrote, "Our work is unique: why confuse it with what is done by everyone else?" He was particularly distressed by any tendency to underplay the importance of F.M. Alexander's four books.

Walter also disliked authoritarianism. He would help anyone who sought his help, but "would not presume to tell anyone how they ought to teach". His firm conviction was that our responsibility as teachers is to support rather than criticize each other.

Those were the reasons for Walter's decision to resign from STAT unless differences could be resolved by the 2005 AGM.

There has been a rumour that teachers who shared Walter's concerns were prejudiced against STAT's becoming a company limited by guarantee. This is quite unfounded, and Walter obviously had no such prejudice (his own Constructive Teaching Centre has always been a limited company, as far as I know). His concerns were quite different: for him, the Technique was a vocation. For seventy years, and literally until his death, Walter was always occupied with the essentials of the Alexander Technique, never with peripheral details.

Jeanne Day

Jeanne: Taking Alexander pupils, students, teachers, all together – in your opinion, what percentage of them really understand what the Technique is about?

Walter: Many realize its value and uniqueness, and many can write and talk about it brilliantly, but only about 3% understand the true significance of inhibition.

Alex Murray

When, in 1934, F.M. Alexander invited Walter Carrington to dinner, he started the chain of events that ensured the growth and development of his Technique.

Meredith Page

After spending the better part of one-and-a-half decades working and learning with Walter, I left London in 1988 to teach and study in Holland. The work was demanding and often daunting and many were the times I lost my inspiration. It was in this state of despair that I received from Walter, a copy of *Thinking Aloud*.

I read the first chapter and felt I had just had the most splendid Alexander lesson of my life. I had been at most of the lectures transcribed in it but, I have to confess, it was only when I met them again, that their incredible power and depth, cloaked as it was in Walter's deceptively simple and concise wording, hit home. My teaching took a remarkable turn for the better.

It seemed that Walter's presence and authenticity had materialised out of the pages, right beside me in my teaching room - totally unimpeded by the restrictions imposed by distance, time and space. It was the same "coherent field of consciousness" of which Brick Bradford had spoken.

Jacob Heringman

I have read Walter's published lectures, and I return to them often. I never cease to marvel at them. They have made me stop and think so many times. I believe that his gift of expressing ideas in a compellingly simple way was a wonderful and tremendous asset, which made his communication so powerful for so many people.

Like lots of other people who didn't know Walter very well, I somehow feel as if I did know him well! It is as if I've lost a friend and teacher. I suppose this is partly true because he shines through in the hands of so many other teachers I've studied with. Like countless others, I shall miss his presence a great deal.

Elizabeth Langford

Immediately on receiving *Thinking Aloud,* I started to read it, without waiting to get up and dress. The echo of Walter's voice caused me at times to laugh aloud in delight, and I didn't get out of bed until I had read the book from cover to cover.

Years later, while reading this and Walter's other books several times a year, it always seems possible to reflect on them with deepening understanding.

Steven Hallmark

Walter was quite pessimistic about people's real desire for change. He sometimes said, "I don't really expect people to listen to me or to remember anything I've said".

Duncan Smart

Isn't it amazing how the tiniest quote, of just a word or two, is unmistakeably Walter? The day I heard he'd died, I went for a long walk with *Thinking Aloud* under my arm, wandered through the ruins of East Berlin until I stumbled onto something out of a 1960's James Bond set, a beach bar laid out among old trees, factory rubble and barbed wire. Having ordered a "Mosquito" cocktail of tonic water, mint, lime and crushed ice, I sat on a couch sculpted out of turf and just quietly read *Thinking Aloud* in the sun. And it struck me how Walter almost never used long words, but deployed short, simple ones in impossibly elegant and appropriate ways.

I remember my first lesson with him: I had just qualified, and was full of confusion about what to do next. Being a fruit (or dropped leaf, or fur-ball) of a conservatoire, I wondered if I should try for employment at a music college, and I asked Walter if he thought it was better to start general teaching first, or go straight into one's speciality. (Duh!)

He pondered quietly for a while – I was sitting at this point, and he had his hand on the back of my neck. After a while, he said, "Well, I think the first thing is to establish where you are, and what the possibilities are".

He got me nicely on to my sitting bones and suddenly I noticed the flowers in the garden, because my eyes had gone into focus. He then said, "Then, what you need to do is quite simply to find out where it is that you want to go". I breathed in, coming up in front. And, as he took me out of the chair, he said, "And go there! There you are! Good man".

And that was the end of that lesson, except of course that I'm still having it, and will be having it for the rest of my life. Walter is still here, very palpably, in that what he brought about in us with his hands is still developing in us. Yes, we go on.

Walter's "oneliners"

Wherever you're going, there's only one place you can start from, and that's where you happen to be.

Well, that's just the way it is. Now let's see where we can go from here.

Life would be no fun at all if we weren't wrong. It would be game, set, and match without having had the fun of playing.

If you become aware that you're stiffening and pulling yourself down, the first thing to do is to say to yourself, "well, that's the way it is".

Everybody is to some degree spastic.

You want to avoid making a bad situation worse.

Only about 3% understand the true significance of inhibition.

What happens when I do nothing?

Going up is like the difference between a hovercraft that's switched on, and one that's not.

Take up your share of space in the world.

If you're going to stretch a piece of string, you don't just pull on one end.

You don't see a lot of snakes with slipped discs.

I do think there is such a thing as the human spirit.

There is one question to ask ourselves: What am I becoming today?

Feelings about oneself can be just as habitual as any mechanical process.

A mental attitude can be practised as well as a physical one.

Some days I say to myself, "It's raining" – and it is.

The core of the Technique lies in not doing what you don't want to do.

You've got to say, "No, this is something different".

Let's see what the situation is. How do I proceed from here?

For heaven's sake, they are your legs!

People often forget that our simple wish is the prime source of all our energy.

on biographies
Memory is idiosyncratic.

to musicians
Way beyond (instrumental) technique is communication with the people you are playing for. If you're free and going up, it will be communicated to the audience.

to new Alexander teachers
Just remember you know a jolly sight more about it than the punter does.

Get your directions going, go into monkey, and put your hands on.

We are all afraid of falling.

Keep your aim and frame it in your mind.

The time is going to come when you are the person who is supposed to know. Read FM's books.

on teaching the Alexander Technique
The Alexander Technique guides one towards the state of freedom and balance of body and mind that is the basis of effective performance in all activities.

This work is about identifying the wrong and allowing the right.

Our work is no better and no worse than what can happen between one teacher and one pupil.

It is no good seeing our work like that of anyone else, because it isn't.

Nothing suffices except showing. You've got to show them.

You've got to find a way to communicate.

You cannot get people to understand unless they have the experience.

If you do potty work you meet potty people.

You'll never get rich, but you'll get tremendous existential satisfaction.

About FM

FM used to say, "It is useless for anyone to try to be right while they are still doing the wrong thing."

For FM, self-regulation was the paramount consideration.

FM used to say, "How can you be sure that you have all the premises for your deductions?"

FM was a very practical man.

About FM's books

There isn't really any other source from which you can get this practical information. Read the books.

Kate Kelly Tanquay

Walter was a man who brought joy into life. For the twenty years I knew him as a student and teacher I don't think there was a day when I saw him that I didn't hear his rich laughter or at least see his beaming smile. He made learning fun with a limerick or a joke to help in the business of going up. There was very little excuse or opportunity to pull down in Walter's presence.

His kindness and generosity of spirit when he was teaching brought out the best in me and he enhanced the quality of my life by being the most marvellous example of living the Technique. Whoever declared, "Too many rules, not enough examples" had never met Walter.

One of the privileges of being around both Walter and Dilys in their seventies and eighties has been to see how they coped with very real changes as they faced into the challenges of growing older. From their example, I have seen how the Technique lends practical grace to illness and aging.

Walter was an insatiable reader. He and Dilys revelled in their visits to the book stores of Hay-on-Wye, and we were introduced to a wonderful selection of books, ranging from The First Ladies' Detective Agency series to the recent edition of the Born-Einstein letters. I miss Walter for our conversations about books. I was so pleased if once in a rare while, I was first to find something of interest to him!

Walter regularly told his students and pupils stories, touching the past, the present and the future. He was a wonderful story-teller. Many, many times, on coming into the class to read from Alexander's books, he would answer an unasked question in my mind by telling us a story. Because these tales were universally applicable, they were meaningful to a lot of his listeners.

I learned about truly being in the present moment from Walter. However short the amount of time spent with him, there never appeared to be any hurry or rush; there was always time enough, because his approach was so focussed on the essence of the Technique. Walter's first-hand knowledge of FM's work, and his respect for FM's writing, meant that his teaching was never diluted for any reason: it was always about restoring my facility to appreciate and apply Inhibition and Direction. I feel profoundly grateful for having benefited so often from those strong and sensitive hands that helped me to become more who I am. Now when I put a hand on a pupil, the reassurance Walter gave me, through his grounded application of principle, abides strongly with me. I only have to read Alexander's books at random and Walter's voice is speaking from the pages. He brought Alexander's life and writing alive with anecdotes and memories, which I treasure and continue to share with others.

At the 2004 Centenary celebration of Alexander's arrival in England, he said of FM, "When he was your teacher you knew you had a friend". He could so easily have been talking about himself. When he called you "My dear" you knew he meant it. Thank you dear Walter for everything, told and untold.

Phyllis Richmond

Overcoming pain

I was in London just before Walter's last hip replacement. He could barely walk; he shuffled from chair to pupil to railing, but he was smiling and upright as ever. When he beckoned me for my turn, I saw him suddenly stop moving completely, as his face blanched. This uncharacteristic moment only lasted a second, then he beamed and gave me a wonderful turn, his big, generous hands and calm demeanor inviting me to go up and up. He did not let the pain or the physical limitation control his way of going or affect his work.

I have had to deal with longstanding problems both from the injuries that brought me to the Technique in the first place and later accidents – always musculo-skeletal injuries, painful and slow to heal, providing lots of incentive to pull down.

About ten years ago I was in a car accident and suffered whiplash down the left side of my neck and shoulder and back. I tried to inhibit and direct but it was so hard to persevere when I could not tell if it was having any effect. For months those muscles shrieked at me! It was very demoralizing.

When I paid my annual visit to Lansdowne Road, Walter was most understanding. He reminded me that soft tissue must have time to heal. In the meantime, he encouraged me to inhibit and direct, even if I could not tell what was going on. This way, as the injury healed, I would be going up and this would help the healing process, whereas if I pulled down, the compression would hinder the healing process and reinforce the cycle of pain. The Alexander Technique does not always take away pain, but we can use ourselves well anyway, and that is always beneficial.

I understood Walter's attitude to be distilled from years of dealing with his World War II hip injuries, repeated deterioration, and hip replacement surgeries. He did not let these problems hinder him or pull him down. He taught until shortly before he died, and he continued to ride his horse Badger until he was in his eighties. In his work, he was always clear, steady, uplifting and inspiring.

Walter taught by example. I have kept his courage and his encouragement in mind through many different varieties of pain. If Walter could overcome it, well then, I will, too.

Glynn Macdonald

This is an extract from the tribute at the Memorial Service. (Ed.)

Glynn Macdonald recorded this the day when Walter said to her:

I'm coming up to 85, I'll be 85 next May. And I have experienced a great deal of change in myself, and of course, as one gets older, the changes with ageing are very interesting and very significant, because life does take on a very different aspect as you get older. And the great deal of the problem with ageing is that you've got such strongly established habits, which, of course, at an advanced age are totally inappropriate. You are trying to do things in the way that you used to do them, but you can't do them like that. But the more you try to do them that way, the more you fail and the more you get into a muddle.

So, it does come back to the same Alexander thing. You've got to stop and you've got to say, "Hang on a minute. Let's see what the situation here is. How do I proceed from here?"

Instead of telling yourself, "Well, I know how to proceed from here. I've been doing this for x number of years", you've got to say, "No, this is something different".

You see "the readiness is all".

George I. Lister

I met Walter during the summer of 2000, when I attended a Teachers' Refresher Course at the Constructive Teaching Centre in Holland Park, London. I had been warned that he would not be teaching this course, as he had done a long year's work, taught the Refresher Course the week before, was 85 years old, and deserved a rest.

He showed up every day.

What a marvelous and unexpected treat! Walter welcomed everyone, taught many private lessons, and each day gave a "turn" to every attendee and teacher on the course. I was captivated as he brought life and energy to Alexander's writings. The atmosphere was one of grace and respect – for the work, for Walter, for the staff teachers, and for each other.

The experience of the Refresher Course gave me a big boost; I came away feeling validated about my teaching, believing I was heading in the right direction. Frequently, seminars or courses leave me a bit skeptical, questioning the value of my time and effort. Not at CTC. Every day was exciting, compelling, and full of dignity and good humor.

I have returned often to Lansdowne Rd., both as a visiting teacher and as a student participating a second time in a Refresher Course. Every journey has included at least one private lesson and many in-class turns with Walter. Through the years I've gotten to know him a bit and value his kindness and gentleness. Although our separations were sometimes many months, he recalled precisely where we had left off.

Most recently in July of this year, I returned to CTC as the director of my own training course. I had scheduled a lesson with Walter, as had my wife Sally (this was to be her first with him). We were disappointed to learn that for health reasons he might need to cancel one or both. Fortunately, he pulled through, was teaching as usual, and made time available for both of us. Sally's scheduled lesson was Thursday, July 21, the day of the failed terrorist attacks. She was delayed on the tube and risked missing this long-awaited opportunity. When I mentioned to Walter that Sally was late, he assured me not to worry, and everyone pulled together to make sure she got her lesson.

Walter and the people associated with him have meant a great deal to me and to my career since we first met five years ago. His work, his presence will continue to be a part of my life, and his talks are required study in the curriculum of my training course. Anyone who has attended the training or Refresher Courses at Lansdowne Road may think of Walter as he enters the main room at noon, sits in the straight-backed wooden chair by the door, and brings us with him as he journeys through Alexander's work. When I read his talks, when we chat about them in my training course class, I am transported to that room. I hear his voice and marvel at the understanding, elegance, and humor with which he approaches this work.

I have been most fortunate to have met, worked with, learned from, and gotten to know a few of the great teachers and inspirations of my profession. Two are now gone – Troup Matthews and Walter Carrington. They leave a legacy which will be a challenge to sustain. I will be forever grateful to have known them.

On a personal note for Sally and me – our reflections on our final lessons with Walter will remain a shared powerful and, at the same time, sad experience. He was only a number of days from his death and his work was clear, compelling and inspiring.

Beret Arcaya

Walter was the most benevolent and kind teacher I ever knew. He was wise and very aware of what his students were going through as they faced the changes this work brings about. He never made any comment about this, leaving much unsaid but all understood.

His teaching always varied with the pupil and the needs of the lesson. He seemed to have a way of helping each one of us reach a quiet and depth within, and he never set himself up as a guru who had "given" us the experience. He possessed a freedom from egoism.

He was always fair-minded and non-judgmental and gave the casual observer the feeling that no request would be turned down. But in fact Walter was fully able to say NO and when he decided NOT to do something he was unshakeable in the decision. Dilys would laugh and call him "pig-headed". He had a delightful sense of humour and during the six years I lived there at the house while I took graduate semesters, I never heard a harsh tone or disparaging word from him, to or about anyone. It is hard not to think of him as nearly saintly because his capacity to be kind seemed to have no limit.

In the final two weeks of the summer term 2005 I had what was to be my last private lesson with him. I felt a special urge that day to thank him for everything, and I told him there were no words to express what he and Dilys had done for me and how grateful I was. Walter had been ill and was very thin. I had been shocked to see him so frail (it had been three months since my last visit) so we were all happy that he was to have some tests and he was given a clean bill of health. All his symptoms were easily explained and a very simple dietary adjustment was in order. We were thrilled, he was very happy and even went out to an end of term dinner party. That weekend he had a fatal fall. He died peacefully two weeks later. His passing marked the end of an era.

I have a mental snapshot of him on his last Friday in class as he motioned me over to give me a turn. Every day I think about him and how he helped me learn such important life lessons.

So his influence never ends for me and I will do my utmost to pass on all he so generously gave.

Rhuna Martin

Walter was for me the embodiment of the Alexander Technique.

He had learned so well the lesson of Inhibition, using it as a means of achieving a wonderful balance between the conscious control of his rational, emotional, and spiritual self.

This enabled him to be the immensely knowledgeable, warm, kindly, and humorous friend so many of us were lucky enough to know. A man of poise and balance, who found such pleasure in so many things.

I loved the pleasure Walter took in good use of words, and the clear lucid way he expressed his thoughts, and occasionally, his own additions to the language. My favourite, when he could not recall a name, was, "My forgettery is working well today".

Being such an astonishingly well-read man, he also had a quotation to suit any eventuality, many of them very amusing, which he would end with that wonderful, wholehearted, infectious laugh.

Walter was able to see people as they could be. He was wonderfully gifted at knowing just how far to take you at that time, never over-extending you in a way you would not be able to sustain. Little by little however, he was enabling change, and gradually you became aware that, apparently by magic, there was a new improved you.

This was not simply a new improved you who could move better and had fewer aches and pains, but a much deeper integrated and stable Self. I felt that in some way I have not experienced with any other teacher, Walter managed to transmit his own deeply peaceful core to those he taught, and this, to me, is what the Alexander Technique is about.

He was able to do this, because he totally lived by the ideas he had learned, and was a living example of their transformative power.

I went for a lesson just after I had been told I had very early cancer. I was absolutely gutted, and faced with several big decisions as to how to proceed.

Walter proceeded as usual with the lesson for a couple of minutes, and then spoke in a way I had not heard him do before.

He said it was important to think what life and living were about; that each day, when we woke, there was only one question to ask ourselves, and that was "What am I becoming today?"

Each day, as we went about our lives, we must keep that thought in mind, and use our directions to facilitate that becoming. He asked me to be particularly mindful of not interfering with breathing, and not allow myself to be invaded by worry.

But mainly to remember that life was about living and becoming until we drew our last breath.

It was the only lesson I had with Walter that left me very tearful, but somehow able to deal with the next difficult weeks. As always, he had known what was needed, and how to deliver it, the mark of a great human being and a wonderful friend. I thought about his words a lot when I saw him in hospital during the last few days of his life.

I knew he had been very ill as a result of the fall, and not able to move much without help. I was delighted, therefore, when he slowly reached his hand out to me. I took it and held it and then realised there was a lot of energy coming from it. He began moving and lengthening his fingers, then moving the arm, and finally extended it up above his head. He then turned to me and said, "Pretty damn good eh?" with a wonderful grin.

I saw that he was putting into practice his advice to me, and living even those last difficult days with the idea of growth and transformation.

Until the day before he died he was his wonderful, lucid, charming self, and able to hold my hand and ask how I was!

How fortunate we have been to have such a friend and teacher.

Walter speaks about Alexander's books

Walter always insisted on the fundamental importance of studying Alexander's four books:

Man's Supreme Inheritance
Constructive Conscious Control of the Individual
The Use of the Self
The Universal Constant in Living

The following talk, given at the Constructive Teaching Centre on March 4, 2005, can be regarded as his message to us all.

Walter Carrington

I'd like to speak to you about why it is so important that you all be familiar with Alexander's books – that you have not only read the books, but that you really have given some thought to what he says, and related, as far as possible, what you read to your own experience. His books were written out of his experience and the Technique arose out of his experience. It was all the result of what he observed. It wasn't a matter of theories that he formulated – ideas out of the air. It was a very practical matter.

The reason why it's so important to know about the books is because there isn't really any other source from which you can get this practical information.

People these days say, "Oh well, the books are all very old, they were all written a long time ago". And yes, it's true, this book was written in 1910. Good heavens! That's nearly 100 years ago! People have been teaching the Technique ever since that time, and surely we must have learned quite a bit in the subsequent hundred years.

And yes, indeed we have, no doubt about it. We've gained a tremendous amount of knowledge and experience. We know vastly more about it all now than he did in 1910. But at the same time, nobody has, to my knowledge, succeeded in writing a book giving an account of the Technique that is any improvement or advance on what he wrote.

Part of the reason is that all of us, when we came as students to learn the Technique, we had lessons from our teachers, we had it all explained to us, but none of us went through a process similar to what Alexander went through himself. That is to say that *he* didn't have a teacher. He didn't have anybody to show him. It was up to his observation and reasoning and so on, to make these discoveries; and the discoveries he made were extraordinarily important.

The basis for these extraordinarily important discoveries was unquestionably as well recognized in 1910 as it is today: that people's postural behaviour is of some importance. It is recognized very well today that the evolutionary story shows how we human beings have arrived at the upright stance and postural co-ordination we have today. In that process, it is self-evident that we walk about on two feet; and if we are going to do that, we have to balance; and if we are going to balance, we need not to be in a little dream, but we need to be consciously aware of what's going on around us.

These are all very simple and obvious things – things that people, in a sense, know, if you put it to them in a theoretical way. They'll say, "Of course I know that! I walk on two legs. Of course it's important how I use my feet!" Nobody's going to deny that. But it's one thing to recognize all of these facts theoretically, but quite another when it comes to considering their implications – what it actually means, for you and me, for our lives, for our individual behaviour. Then it's a very different matter. And, of course, that is what Alexander found himself, and that is what he set about doing his best to show us and tell us.

In very, very simple terms, you might say in almost caricature terms – there is obviously so much more to it than this – Alexander's problem was that he was losing his voice and he couldn't speak properly. He was stiffening his neck; he was pulling his head back; he was pulling himself down. The problem was then how to stop doing it, and to get familiar with the implications of the whole observation that stiffening the neck, pulling the head back, pulling down was a bad thing. And that it was a good thing, if you could manage, on the other hand, to keep your neck free and keep your head going forward and up and so on and so forth.

Now, he realized from the beginning that if he was going to communicate his solution to the problem, he had to try to explain it to people and show them both the problem and the solution. He had to communicate these things in a way they could understand. And that was as big a difficulty in his day as it is today. Or let me put it the other way around: it's as big a difficulty today as it was in his day. The difficulty has never changed. I've been teaching for quite a long time, and when I meet somebody who comes in to see me for a first lesson, it's no different now to my experience of giving a first lesson sixty years ago. And I'm sure that my experience of giving a first lesson sixty years ago was no different to Alexander's in 1894. The difficulty is the same – always the same.

And quite simply, we've found, over that time, that it's all very well talking to people, it's all very well reasoning with them, it's all very well putting it into words – nothing suffices except showing. You've got to show them. You've got somehow or another to give them the experience. And the words that you use, well, you'll find that the best thing to do is to choose words that your pupils understand. It's no good deciding that you're going to use some verbal formula of words that are totally unfamiliar to them. You've got to find a way to communicate, and I think that *that,* always, will be the difficulty. You cannot communicate this work, you cannot get people to understand, unless they have the experience.

There's nothing short of the experience that will enable people to understand. Yes, you've got to, as a teacher you've got to get people's agreement to accept the experience. A lot of people stop short of that. They don't want the experience; they're afraid of the experience. Seriously! They're afraid of the implications. Something inside them says, "If I really experience this, I'd know something that might make me feel that it was necessary to change. And I don't want to do that, I don't want to know!" And people come to you as pupils; they come for an interview or to enquire about the Technique, so you would think they would want to know. But it isn't by any means as simple as that. Some people, yes, some people are really ready to know and want to know, but there are other people who have managed to persuade themselves that they want to know, but in their heart of hearts they don't want to know at all.

So we do have an awful lot of real difficulties, and what I'm saying is that the difficulties haven't really changed very much since Alexander first started to teach. The daily difficulties I find myself are described in Alexander's own writings. What he refers to is something that in teaching we encounter time and time again. I find it very useful, very helpful, very important to read his thoughts about it, and his experience, how he confronted these difficulties and how he worked out a way of dealing with them. That's some of the reason why I'd recommend that everybody read Alexander's books, but not only read them but really make an effort to understand and think about what he wrote. I suggest that you take what he says as the basis for a little experiment of your own, to see whether things work out the way he said. "Yes, that's what he said, he said it would work out like that. Let's try it and see. Let's give it a go. Let's see if things do work out in accordance with what he said."

Now from a practical point of view, the first training course was the first time that he had ever really set about formally training students to be teachers. He'd trained various people on an apprenticeship basis, but apprenticeship is a little different. He was going to have a number of people coming together on the training course, men and women from all sorts of different backgrounds and experiences, and he wanted above all to try to ensure that these people got the necessary experience from which they would be able to derive the necessary understanding. So he knew that he must work on them individually. Although there was a group of people, the group didn't eliminate the individual element. It was always you, the individual pupil, FM and you. It was between you and him. It didn't matter how many people were in the group, it was always individual – it was you and him! He recognized that very clearly: "That's what I must do!" As I recognize it now. As I sit here, I know it would be absolutely futile to try to work as though you were all the same, or anything like that. You can't help people, you can't give an experience that way. It's got to be, of course, it has got to be individual.

So knowing all of that, he decided to write up an account of how he developed the Technique – the process he'd gone through. He thought he'd do his best to get it down on paper. So he wrote *The Use of the Self* – particularly the chapter called "Evolution of a Technique", which he thought he could give to the students. They'd have their classes, they'd have all the daily practical work, and they'd have this written record to refer to that would help people very much: it would guide people in their thinking to a clearer understanding of what it was all about. That was his idea in writing *The Use of the Self.* His other books were written, not just with his students in view, but as an attempt to reach anybody out there, anybody in the audience who would listen. And he worked very hard in choosing his words to make them as intelligible as possible.

Now, of course, while he was alive, Alexander was always the resource. If people had read his books and didn't understand what he was saying, or indeed if they'd had lessons and they didn't understand, they could always go to him and get the whole explanation from him. When we were working on the training course – I was teaching on the training course while he was alive – I always had the happy thought that he was there. If there were any problems, I didn't have to worry about them too much, because I could refer them to him. He could deal with it. I could get on with teaching, as best I could. I knew my own limitations, and I knew that I didn't know all the answers, but he was there, so I was not going to worry at all! But of course when he died, all of a sudden there you were, you couldn't go and ask him any more. The only way in which we could know what he might have thought was to go and read his books, because we knew he'd done his best in the books to be as clear as possible, and comprehensive. But that was that.

So suddenly, from not having had any responsibility, suddenly I was responsible for the training course. Here was the responsibility – and it was mine. And I thought, well, I'd better read the books to people, because it's all very well saying to people, just as I've been saying to you now this morning, "Read the books". It isn't an easy task. It isn't easy at all! And these days, after all, for a lot of you English isn't your first language, so I'm really making quite a demand in saying, "Read the books". I know how difficult it is.

Of course, I do read them to you on the training course, as I've been reading them to you today. We have come nearly to the end of *Man's Supreme Inheritance*, to this chapter on "Notes and Instances". There is much here that is difficult to understand. If it isn't explained to you, if there isn't somebody to say, "Well, this is what it's about; this is what it really means", you will find it extremely difficult to understand by yourselves. Very largely this is because what he wrote and what he thought was what he had experienced up to 1910. We can now draw on what people have experienced almost up to 2010, and yes, our experience does enable us to define, to describe and clarify a great deal. We now know certain things very clearly and positively about the Technique, which were known only rather vaguely in 1910.

So you do need to have the books read to you by somebody who has got some of the necessary experience, and you do also need to read them and know them yourself. Because you may well find one day that, like me, you haven't felt any overwhelming responsibility and so on – you've felt, "Well, they don't have to ask me; they can go and ask somebody who really knows". But the time is going to come when you are the person who is supposed to know. What I'm saying to you is that you might as well face that in good time and prepare for it, so that you are sure, as far as possible, that you will be able to answer some of the questions put to you when that time comes. There we are. I think that will do.

Congress Lectures (Oxford, 2004)

During the 2004 International Alexander Technique Congress in Oxford, in addition to his Keynote Address, which is published in the Congress Papers, Walter gave a series of three lectures. The first was unfortunately lost when recording equipment failed. The other two are published here for the first time.

At the beginning of each lecture, Walter recapitulated the essence of the previous one, thus ensuring that we all can follow the line of his thought. The last lecture includes Walter's answer to a question that is uppermost in many teachers' minds: how can Alexander teachers succeed in the modern world?

Here again, we can see Walter's consideration for others. Aware that English was not the first language of everyone present, he sometimes made a point of expressing an idea in several different ways.

These lectures, transcribed from DVDs made by Nick Erickson, are published by kind permission of the Carrington family. (Ed.)

Inhibition and Direction

Good morning, everybody. Now first of all, I think I'd better just recap a little bit. I was saying the other day that there are three essential elements, three essential things to think about in connection with our Technique. The first, you and I call *inhibition,* which is a rather frightening word for a lot of people - never mind, ourselves, we know what that means. And then, of course, there's *direction,* and that's what I'm going to speak about a great deal more this morning. And then, of course, the third one is the very important one of what we mean by *giving consent.* So, three things: inhibition, direction, giving consent. That's what it all boils down to.

Yesterday, I spoke about the work of Ben Libet, the scientific work that bears particularly on this matter of the inhibition. What I was really particularly explaining was that people overlook the importance of what we call *the subconscious.* People are familiar with some aspects of this; but of course, mostly, the ordinary man in the street thinks, *Well, I'm either conscious, I'm awake, I know what's going on, or I'm asleep, or I'm unconscious* - and that's it. They're not aware of the immense amount of activity going on in the brain, in the whole sensorium, everything to do with feeling, senses, and so on. And this is what is so relevant to this question of leaving yourself alone, inhibition. If you've got things on your mind, if as I stood here I were thinking, *Oh, I never made that telephone call,* or *I wonder whether I shall get that letter by the next post,* or something like that - if something was bugging me in that way, I'd only *partly* be thinking what I'm saying to you, and I'd easily not choose the right words - it would put me off.

No. For conscious performance, it is very, very important that inhibition should work, so that one can be focussed in present time. But I think you all know that – I don't think I need elaborate on that.

What I wanted to say this morning was that of course if you look at the story of Alexander and his research, his personal research, his work on himself, the very significant feature was his use of the mirror. And the mirror was significant because of course that was really the way into this inhibition, this prevention of interference, this non-doing. I mean, when Alexander stood in front of the mirrors, and looked at himself, he was looking at – so to speak – *another person, there*. He totally forgot *this person here*. He wasn't interested in *this* person, here, his whole interest and attention was on *that* person, there. So, thoughts and feelings, arising from within, were automatically ignored. He wasn't in any way, as he looked at his *alter ego*, as he looked at his image *there*, he wasn't *feeling* what was happening. He was *seeing* what was happening, he was observing in the present moment, in the here and now, and what he was observing was what he could see, *there*.

People very often ask me, "Well, Alexander benefited so much from mirror work. Wouldn't it be a nice idea, shouldn't I do some mirror work? Ought I not to go and stand in front of a mirror and start looking at myself?" And I always have to hesitate in answering that, and look at the person who is asking me, and try and guess how far they would really be able to look in the mirror in the way that Alexander looked. What I mean is, you've got to remember that Alexander was an actor. Of course he'd studied gesture and make-up and all the things that actors have to take into consideration, and for which they use mirrors. So he was quite used to using a mirror as a working tool, to observe and see what was going on.

But you see, you and me, we go and stand in front of a mirror, and we say, *Look at that, my hair's untidy. I've got a smut on my nose. I don't look so good this morning.* And so on. That's the first thing. And of course, what immediately follows from that is, *Well, I'd better do something about my hair. I'm going to straighten my tie. I'm going to do* – whatever it is. So of course, instead of the mirror being a stimulus leading people to leave themselves alone – to non-doing – for many people it's a very powerful stimulus to *do*. Of course, people don't need much encouragement to *do*! So when they then start thinking about Alexander, probably the first thing is, *I'm supposed to go up, aren't I? My head's supposed to go forward and up. I'm standing here. I want my neck to be free; I want my head to go forward and up. I can't really tell whether my neck is free, which is rather worrying. So I'm worried about that, to start with! Then there's this business of my head going forward and up. Well, I've been shown often enough, but let me see, how does it go? Where does it go? What does it look like?* And people, of course, start trying to put their heads forward and up.

So the whole attitude, the whole mental process, the whole approach is totally at variance with what we want. It really is a big trap for young players. It is very, very easy to fall into. People think, somehow or other, *Alexander used the mirror, I ought to use the mirror, a mirror it would be a good idea* – and so on. And then they get themselves into this mess, using the mirror.

So from a teaching point of view, you must warn people about mirrors. You can warn them; whether they'll take any notice of the warning is another matter! But you can say to them, "As you look in the mirror, if you see anything happen, then stop a bit, because it shouldn't."

You can say straight away, "If you can see anything happen, it's wrong!"

So, what we need is to give people the experience of leaving themselves alone, of just – as I was saying yesterday – being in the present moment. You can tell them, "Quite simply, say to yourself, *Where am I?* When you stop and consider *where am I*, then you look out and you see your surroundings, and you're not concerned with yourself. And of course, as soon as you attend to your surroundings, you've got the orientation, you've got the basic direction. And the direction, of course, is: Up."

Now, Alexander, of course, found that the direction was Up, because experiment led him to discover that his voice and his breathing worked more freely and more efficiently when he was up. Or, to put it another way, when he *wasn't* up – when he tightened, when he stiffened, when he pulled his head back, when he pulled down – then of course there was evident strain on his voice. It was a matter of experiment to discover the required direction. At the same time, it wasn't such a difficult observation to make, because quite clearly anybody knows where up is and anybody knows where down is.

Now, from the point of view of our work, it's all very well talking about *up* and *down*, but what about when people are not in the vertical, when they're in the horizontal? What about when they are lying down, for instance?

You see, from the scientific point of view, anthropology – physical anthropology – came up with the observation, the recognition, years ago, that the main characteristic of us human beings – *homo sapiens sapiens*, our kind – the major characteristic of our kind was what was called "orthograde posture".

Now, orthograde means "standing straight". In 1902, shortly before Alexander arrived in England, Sir Arthur Keith, who was a great anthropologist, a great expert in these things, said that the necessary orthograde posture meant the uprightness of the spinal axis. So the characteristic of the human being is *fully upright with the axis of the spine in the vertical.* Well, of course that's a fair enough description of somebody standing on two feet and letting the postural mechanism work and leaving himself alone. We can quite understand that, of course. Among ourselves, certainly, when I was a student on Alexander's training course - and I suppose in the training course before my time - we all talked about "keeping the length". And we would look at one another and we'd say, "Go up. You're not keeping your length; you're shortening; you're pulling down. You've got to keep your length". We had this idea of length, of full uprightness, and we'd realized by experiment, by experience, that you didn't get satisfactory length, that the attitude was not satisfactory if you stiffened and tensed to do it. Well, it couldn't be, really, because, of course, if you were really trying to *hold* yourself up - if you were constantly making an effort to stand up straight, to "stand tall" and so on - if you were consciously doing that, you were making a lot of muscular effort. And muscular effort means contraction - that's how muscles work. So even if we couldn't observe it, we could be sure that muscles were contracting and working quite hard in order to achieve this supposedly desirable result of standing straight, standing tall.

When you see how the guardsmen stand, when you think of soldiers on parade, it's the result of a great deal of muscular effort, which is quite contrary to what we want. We are talking about what Professor Raymond

Dart described very simply and nicely when he talked about "the attainment of poise". Now somehow, *poise* is not a word that we warm to at once. Somehow "poise" has come to mean *a little bit contrived, a bit artificial.* It shouldn't. It should really mean that we have got that natural freedom that is what our endowment entitles us to. And that is the full length, the full height, the full freedom, the full mobility. So there is our aim; that is what we have in mind. That is what we need.

But now there are two considerations. First of all, we are not in the vertical all the time. What about when we lie down? What about other attitudes? Well, keeping the length is still the requirement; it's just as much a requirement in one attitude as in another. It doesn't matter how the body is in space, whether it's horizontal or vertical, so long as you've got the length, it will be fine.

This may seem strange at first, until you begin to consider. And when you do consider, you will realize that all vertebrates – all creatures with spines – of course they all have a basic need: the need to feed; the need to find food. So the problem is to get the mouth connected with the food.

When a baby is born, almost the first thing that happens as soon as it arrives out of the womb, as soon as it's overcome the shock, the first thing is, *Where's the grub?* The newborn baby has the equipment, right from birth, to find the source of food. It's very obvious in animals. It's probably more simply seen in the birth of a foal or a calf or something like that. It's quite remarkable; they get up on their knees and they look for their mother and for the teat. In the human baby it's not quite so obvious – although it's pretty obvious to mum! I think she knows all about it.

Now the fact that the mouth must find the way means that everything has got to co-ordinate so that that can happen. The head leads, yes, we can say that the head leads. But the tongue leads; the tip of the tongue leads. The tip of the tongue is the most important recognition instrument for finding where that food is. In the search for the food, the tongue goes forward in the mouth.

The tongue, as you know, is attached to this bone under the angle of the jaw, called the hyoid bone. The hyoid bone has the larynx – the voice box – attached to it. And attached to that are the collar-bone, the breastbone, and so on, right the way down the front. So you've got the tip of the tongue at one end, and you've got all this connection of muscles and bones and everything that go right through the whole body. Of course I'm speaking about the human body at the present moment, but the general argument of what I'm saying is that in vertebrates – if you like, in snakes, for instance – it's the mouth, the tip of the tongue, that has to find the food. The whole body has to work freely, has to mobilize, has to do what is necessary to allow that to happen.

So, there's no question about it at all, in whatever attitude a human being finds himself – whatever the orientation, vertical or horizontal or anything in between – what matters is keeping the length, keeping the spine so that the spinal joints are free, so that there's no more muscular effort going on than is absolutely necessary. But of course there is a great deal of muscular effort required, a great deal of fine tuning, a great deal of delicacy, to maintain the mobility of one bone to the other, of one part to another. When you look into all that, it's inconceivably complicated. But, of course, in looking through this complication, you can see the simplicity of it. It is, as Magnus said years ago, it is the head leading and the body following.

Now one point I'd like to mention is this. I think what I've said so far is all common sense. I don't think anybody will strongly disagree with what I've said. But you know, all the health professionals, all the medics and so on: yes, they know all this too; they recognize it too – but do they think it has any importance? Very, very little! Yes, they examine people. They find perhaps that the heart is irregular, or the digestion is unsatisfactory – whatever their diagnostic tests come up with. Although they look at specific function – cardiac function, respiratory function, and so on – they never look at what we can probably describe as the postural function. They never look at what I've been talking about, never consider that. Perhaps, as the examination finishes, as you go out of the room, they might say, "Your posture's terrible; you ought to do something about it. Why don't you do some decent walking, or go to the gym or something?" But that is as far as it ever goes.

And it is an extraordinary thing in this day and age, when Alexander's original observations were made over a hundred years ago. Here we are, celebrating the centenary of his arrival in England – and 1894 is the date that we now view as the sort of starting-point. Isn't it extraordinary to think that in all that time this obvious fact has not really percolated? And of course that brings me back to what I said the other night. If any of you heard me, on Monday night I quoted Niels Bohr, who was saying that of course in science, the great discovery, the major discovery, is not recognized at first. It is only half understood even by the people who made the discovery.

So it's not surprising, so we might as well be patient about this and carry on quietly. Yes, patience! Not to do anything, not to address head on this problem that I've outlined. You will not succeed in persuading people of the truth that we are speaking about, until they get some taste of the experience. Without the experience, they simply will not understand. You may think, you may believe, that if you can explain it yourself now, in words that are crystal clear, sentences that have been so carefully constructed that you are sure that they say what you intended to say, that they convey your meaning – *Here it is!* – and you put it in front of them. Without the experience, it's nothing – it is NOTHING.

And you've got to remember, in your own use of yourself, that when you have made all this effort to try and convince people, to try and explain to people, and you find that you are not getting through at all – what is your reaction? Well, the reaction is disappointment, frustration. And how do you react to disappointment and frustration? You try harder. And you get into a worse mess! You try harder and they look at you and they say "Well, *you*'ve got a bee in your bonnet all right, haven't you? Yes, of course I can understand how keen you are on this Alexander thing. But of course it's just your own enthusiasm, it's just not really rational." So please remember that, and apply the Technique in that connection.

And that leads me to a further very important thing that I would like to point out to you. In these days, a lot of Alexander people – by which I mean both teachers and experienced students – are very interested in exploring what they call the scientific aspects of the Technique, the underlying physiology, the underlying anatomy. How does it all work? Very reasonable, you can quite understand it. We all have a curiosity; we all want to know these things; we all *like* to know these things. I'm not suggesting for a moment that there's anything wrong with that curiosity.

But what people very often overlook is that the nature of science is to explain how things work. Scientists are seeking explanations of how things work. And indeed, with all their apparatus and all the advances that have been made, people are now able to give remarkably detailed descriptions of how things work. Of course, we all have to acknowledge – *they* have to acknowledge – that the amount we know, though it may be quite a lot, it is still partial, a fraction of what there is to find out. So they're going to keep at it; they're not going to be satisfied with the present knowledge. They're looking for more, of course. And again, it's all perfectly reasonable.

But you see, when we study how things work, what is our attitude, what is our reaction to this knowledge? We look, and we say that it is not working according to the description! We can see lots of things wrong, according to this knowledge that we've got. We can see that somehow these muscles – that the physiologists tell us are supposed to do this or that – are either atrophied or hypertrophied, either doing too little or too much. And of course the result is that we don't have the free natural movement of the hand or the arm or the foot, or some other part of the body. Or the breathing – if you like – doesn't work according to the textbook, according to the description of how the scientists have established that it ought to work. And how do we react to that? Well, of course, that is a very, very powerful stimulus to try and make it happen. That is really going to set you on the path of trying to *do* something. Here it isn't working, so you are going to *do something to make it work*. Well, you can imagine the trouble you can get into that way!

Science isn't about that. We come to technology; we come to engineering. Now, the engineer has an engine. The engine has been constructed and put together and tested, and it works. And the engineer looks at it and he says, *yes, but the valve timing isn't quite right,* or *this bearing is a little bit slack.* The engineer looks – not saying he knows how the machine is supposed to work – but he knows what is wrong when he looks at it. When you take your car for service to the garage, you hope that the chap who services it will look to see what's wrong with it. He may have tremendous knowledge of how it's all supposed to be, of how it's all supposed to work, and that's just fine, but that's not his concern. His concern is *spotting what's wrong,* and then, of course, making the correction.

We, similarly, should be looking at ourselves and at others, all the time in terms of trying to figure out what's wrong. And when we've established what's wrong, then to prevent it. To prevent it. Like the engineer servicing the motor vehicle. He takes it for granted that the thing was put together correctly, that it was constructed in such a way that it would work as it's supposed to work. He is looking to trace the fault – to trace the wrong thing and to see, then, what he can do to put it right. We, in our case, we have to rely on Nature to put things that are wrong, right. It's the force of Nature, the energy of Nature that takes us up, that mobilizes us, that enables us to do all the things that we have been speaking about. So, of course, it is – quite simply and practically speaking – *a matter, for us, of prevention.*

So let us not forget it, when we come to study the science of things – fascinating as that is, and I'm not in any way saying a word against it; the more we know, the better. The more we know, the more we can benefit, and can benefit our pupils with our greater understanding. But from a practical point of view, remember that the task is, *not to do.* It's not to make something happen, it's not to push yourself up, it's not to put your head forward and up, it's not to lengthen in a positive sense.

It is to prevent what will hinder Nature from the natural flow of energy that takes us up and supports us – and that flow of energy is as necessary whether we are in the horizontal or the vertical. It makes no difference. You still want to have – as we say, quite simply – the length, you still want to have the spine mobilized so that you have freedom in the joints. Clearly, when you're lying down, the whole structure is not weight-bearing, so there's a great deal less demand, a great deal less activity. But at the same time, the requirement is the same: it is getting the length and keeping the length that frees you. So that is a matter of prevention.

We often say that the underlying concern, the underlying principle of our work is prevention. And that, of course, is what we have to try and teach our pupils, to show them how they can prevent, by first of all stopping – coming into the present, recognizing where they are, recognizing the situation, knowing where up is, so to speak. And then, of course – with that recognition – in order to prevent, you have to become aware of the interference. FM had to research for some time before he discovered that it was, after all, the pulling back of his head, and the raising of his chest, and that thing about taking hold of the floor with his feet – you remember. All sorts of things he gradually discovered he was doing wrong, and the requirement was: to prevent it. And when he succeeded in preventing it, the whole thing worked very, very much better.

I referred to his work in front of the mirrors. It was, as you remember, his voice and his breathing that he found he needed to focus on. That gave him something very positive – he had really quite a lot of big problems – to work on.

When he came to study the breathing, he found how inadequately people breathe, how limited their breath capacity was. And at first, for ten years of his teaching, his main focus was on preventing interference with the breathing, preventing interference with those processes that allow the full opening out of the ribcage, the whole opening out of the breathing apparatus. For want of a better term, he called it "full chest breathing". If you'd asked people in 1910 - yes, even as late as 1910 - what Alexander was after, they'd have replied, "full chest breathing": that people could breathe in such a way that they used the whole breathing mechanism, that they had the resources available to them. It was a matter of releasing and freeing and not doing the wrong thing.

Of course, the improvement in the breathing - brought about by the improvement in the whole working of the postural mechanism, the whole matter of poise - led to an improvement in the whole organism. And very soon after that time, he came to have pupils who were not primarily concerned about their voice, not primarily concerned about breathing, but who had problems with back pain, and with ticks and nervous manifestations of one sort or another, or arthritic conditions; interference with the circulation, with the digestion - you name it, any sort of functioning. Because all these things, of course, are posturally related. And as we know, if we can manage to bring about an improvement in respiration - an improvement, in the way *this* work leads to improvement - then of course it will all expand, it will all develop.

As far as you and I are concerned, we are quite familiar with the idea, we are quite comfortable with the phrase, *general functioning*. We can say about someone, "Oh, their general functioning is pretty good", or "their general functioning is pretty rotten".

General functioning, to us, is a fairly obvious concept that does not need very much explanation. We take it for granted that the human organism functions as a whole. What a contrast with the so-called *scientific medicine*, with the scientific approach, which has no concept whatever of general functioning! Specific functioning, yes, specific functioning of the heart, of the lungs, and so on – they know a vast amount about *specific* functioning. But how one function relates to another is something they're not interested in. The specialists are too busy with their specialization to expand their thought and observation to embrace a concept of *general* functioning.

So these are the problems that we have in our teaching, these are the problems that we come across in our daily life. Whether we are dealing with health professionals, whether we are dealing with laymen, it makes no matter: they all have exactly the same problems as you and me. The doctor, the consultant who knows so much and can give you valuable advice about your heart function – as he sets about his work and as he advises you, look how he's sitting in the chair, look how he's breathing. Notice what his use of his voice is like. And look at the amount of tension, look at his head and neck, when he wants to get a point across to you, when he says, "You must take this medication. It's no good messing about. If you don't take this medication, I tell you, you'll have a heart attack. You've got to do it". While he's making the point, how's he doing it? *(Here, Walter mimed the way most people use themselves when being emphatic.)* We're all familiar with that, and of course, you can't turn round and say, "Hang on, Doctor; wait a minute".

But having recognized that, and bearing it in mind, for heaven's sake, don't neglect his advice! Don't despise his advice because you look at him and you think,

"Well, he's not such a wonderful specimen". He's got tremendous specific knowledge that you haven't got. But do just remember, *do remember* to keep in present time, to keep aware of your surroundings, paying attention to what is happening around you rather than paying attention to what you are feeling inside! Be aware of the question *Where am I?* and that the answer is *Here. And where do I wish to be? I wish to be expanding, I wish to be there.*

I think that will do for this morning.

First, I'd better just re-cap for a moment, and recall to your attention that I'm dealing with three very simple things. First of all, what we call the Inhibition - beastly word, but there it is. It means stop. But it means more than stop: it means ask yourself where you are; realize your surroundings; come into present time; stop thinking about the future or about other things; focus your attention on the present. And when you've come into the present, then the question of Direction will be obvious; because when you know where your surroundings are, then, of course, you definitely know where Up is.

When you know where Up is, the next serious consideration is: how much or how little do you wish to go there? Because if you don't wish to go there very much, you probably won't go there very much. If you really wish to go there quite a lot, it can have most surprising results. I was talking about all that previously.

Now, what I want to talk about a little more specifically this morning is the matter of direction itself, because, as I say, when you come into the present, and you look around you, the direction is somewhere up there, but you don't know *precisely* the direction. You don't know Up in the sense that you would need to know where Up is to balance yourself.

Up, of course, plays a vitally important part in our use of ourselves. Quite simply, the underlying mechanism - the underlying neurology and physiology - works to support us and take us up. Some of you might have been at Paul Burge's lecture yesterday morning, when of course he was talking particularly about voice. All voice users hear the phrase, *support the voice*, or *support the breath*. They are all fairly familiar with the idea that the voice, the breath, needs to be supported.

But where does the support come from? Support does not come from the diaphragm, it doesn't come from anywhere else except the floor. It comes from the ground, it comes from your feet; everything in the way of support comes from your feet. It is the contact of the feet on the floor that activates the whole support process to prevent you from falling over, to enable you to move, to enable you to be up. Of course, when you come to think about it, you will recognize why human beings are supposed to be fully upright, or as the scientists say, orthograde. ("Orthograde", meaning "standing straight up".)

What is the significance of *straight up*? Well, of course, it's that straight up is the easiest way to balance. If you are not straight up, if you are over to one side or another, more effort is going to be required to support you and take you up. But if you find *straight up*, if you find the direction *straight up*, then that gives you the best possibility of free support without having to make a great deal of tension and effort. That's why we think in terms of the head going forward and up, and, of course, the back lengthening and widening and so on.

But the essence of the matter is, *freely, straight up*. Not stiff straight up, not push straight up, but free straight up. And then up.

Now here is something that I very often tell our students these days. Some of them seem to find that this is an idea that is helpful. So I say to you now, talking of Direction, talking of Up, here you all are sitting here, would you know where North is? Would you know the compass direction? In this large building, with the distances you have to walk, you might be not quite sure, in this room, where North is. So what shall we do about it? Let's get a magnetic compass. Let's put the compass somewhere on the table or on the floor and let it quietly settle down. And let's make sure that we haven't got anything to disturb the magnetic field like a great big penknife in our pockets or something like that. Here is the needle swinging, and quietly settling down, and it will point to magnetic north. So now we know, fairly precisely, where magnetic north is, by use of the compass.

Now what I want to point out to you is that here, for instance, we stand upright or find a degree of uprightness as we sit. We don't stiffen our necks; we allow the head to be freely poised; the head is not pulled backwards or forwards or on to one side: it's poised, it's balanced - it's pivoted, if you like - on the end of the spine. Now our head works very, very similarly to a magnetic compass; in this sense, that our head knows where up is. It not only knows in general terms, but it knows in precise terms, it registers the direction of up. So, if your neck is free and you are allowing your head to go forward and up, the direction in which it goes will be quite precise - in terms of your condition and the world around you - at identifying the direction of up. So remind yourself that when it comes to stopping and checking your direction, it makes sense to stop what you are doing for the moment, to make sure that there's nothing interfering with the balance of your head and your neck. If that is all free, then you've got the direction. That is where you want to go. That is where you need to go.

I think it's a very useful thought to bear in mind, because the common difficulty is that even when we have found the direction, when we have determined where we need to go to be up and so on, we so easily think of something else, and we forget it and we lose it. Now if you are sailing a ship or flying an aeroplane, you need to check the compass frequently. You've got to keep your eye on the compass. The person flying or sailing watches the compass fairly regularly, to see that the direction is being maintained. And I suggest to you that that is what we all require to be doing for ourselves in our daily lives, in our daily activity: coming back and checking the compass fairly frequently, to make sure that we are still going in that direction.

Because of course you remember that the last book of Alexander is called *The Universal Constant in Living*. What was the Constant? The constant thing of all was the direction, that continuous process, ensuring that the support was taking us up, so that we were free, we were poised, we were truly orthograde, if you like - to use a scientific term.

When you watch, in this Congress, if you go around and exchange work, and watch the workshops and so on, you will see of course that people are so intent on this that and the other, on going into monkey, on using the feet - on whatever, all the various things we do - that very often they get so much involved in the particular thing they are thinking about - the whispered AH for instance, the smile, you know, *am I really letting my jaw drop freely?* and so on - all these sort of things, yes, but what about the direction? You'd better check the compass while you're thinking about these things. Yes, of course they are quite important, all part of the procedure. But you are sailing the ship, and the ship needs to stay on course. It's not going to stay on course if you don't check the compass, so make sure you check the compass every now and then, whatever you're doing, and don't allow your attention to stray on to *Oh,what am I doing with my feet, what am I doing with my knees, what am*

I doing with my hips? It's all very important, provided that while you check it, you are still on course – that direction is still working. And so there you are, checking the compass.

I think I've made the point clearly enough – I hope so. I don't want to labour it any more, but it is, of course, a very important point to consider.

Just to go one step further, I would say that it's all very well checking the compass, being on course, knowing you're on course – but how long is the journey going to take you? *(laughter)* It's a good question. You either need a fair wind, or you're going to need a bit of power from the engine. It's got to be either one or the other. You've got to have what they call technically *motive power*. And, as I said in the previous talk, motive power comes – according to FM himself – it comes from direction. He says, "When I use the word direction in connection with my use, I implicate the wish, the necessary energy". You see, the direction produces the energy. You've got to allow that energy to work. You've got to do more than *allow* it, you've got to *wish* it, you've got to wish to go somewhere, you've got to wish – and very positively and definitely. It's not *Yes you're on course and you may get there one day.* You want to get there as fast as conditions will allow you to get there. So it is a very, very positive wish to go up.

First of all you've got to identify the direction, but then, finally, you've got to wish to go there. And when you wish to go there, you must take care, make sure that you don't let *doing* come into it. Make sure that you don't supplement the natural flow of energy by some misconceived effort on your part – stiffening, tightening, pushing, or whatever.

So there we are. Direction, wishing, preventing. That's the requirement, that's the simple story.

Well, I think now I'm going to tell you a little story that comes really from the work of a very famous professor at this University. Dr C.D. Darlington was professor of Biology I think – I'm not absolutely certain about that, but I'm quite certain that he was a great authority on plant growth and development, on the early development of the science of genetics, plant breeding and all that kind of thing. And he wrote a book that some of you may know, but if you haven't come across it, I can recommend it. It's called *The Evolution of Man and Society*. I take this story from his book.

Once upon a time there was a tribe somewhere in Africa. They were nomads. That is to say, they didn't have any fixed abode; they lived in tents and shelters that they made, and they lived from what they could gather and what they could hunt. They were nomadic hunter-gatherers, and they moved around and were all very busy and happy keeping themselves alive under the African sun. Now among the tribe of course there were people who were expert in different things, and one of the very important experts was what we should call the Bard. He was the man who knew the history of the tribe, he remembered all the past events, he remembered the stories, and when everybody was gathered together in the evening, or for some festival or whatever, the Bard would be called upon, and he would stand up and tell everybody the old stories and remind them of the history of the tribe. Well, the tribe of course appreciated this very much. What shall we say about it? First of all, the Bard had to know how to use his voice so that everybody could hear him. Because if people at the back couldn't hear him, they got rather cross about it and they'd start jumping up and down. So yes, the Bard knew how to use his voice and that meant he knew how to breathe, and that meant, as we know, that he must have used himself pretty well. He could not have projected his voice and done everything he had to do, if he had rotten bad use. In addition to which, of course, he had a good memory. That was the other main requirement of his job. He had to remember things, he'd got to have some facility with words, he'd got to make himself heard. So he was a very important man, and so long as the tribe had him, everybody was quite content and happy.

Time passed, and they got rather tired of living in tents; they got the idea of more permanent shelters. Mud huts then began to be invented. So: settled places of living, communities, towns. And along with that - as we would say - urban development, people were now going in for more settled agriculture and stock-breeding, and the domestication of animals. And as all that went on, the next thing that developed, obviously, was trade. People who specialized in sheep wanted to be able to swap some sheep for some corn. I don't have to elaborate - you can see quite clearly what I'm talking about. But Darlington points out that when trade first developed, the big problem was in remembering the deals that were being struck; what had been done in the way of *Yes, last week I sold you my favourite cow; you were going to let me have so many bushels of wheat. How many bushels was it? I think it was five, you say it was four. We shouldn't need to rely on our memory; we need to find some other way of being more accurate.*

Some brilliant fellow got the idea of making a clay tablet and got a pointed tool, or a piece of straw, and started making marks on the clay. And so, writing was invented. People who could write were very much in demand. It smoothed the path of commerce. So this was all fine, but when we compare what the scribes were doing with what the bards were doing, the scribes had got these tablets here, and they were doing it all here like this *(here Walter mimed bending over close work)* and of course they didn't have to project their voices, they didn't have to breathe deeply, or speak specially clearly, they were all intent on this. In other words, they were starting to pull themselves down. And of course, you can be absolutely certain that whereas the bards in their trade couldn't afford to pull themselves down, for scribes it didn't matter. So scribes were obviously the first customers that we can identify as clients for the Alexander Technique!

So that was Darlington's story – and my story for today. I think it says quite a lot and is worth bearing in mind and thinking about, because it's what people have forgotten as our society has developed. As our conditions of life have developed, we have lost those essential requirements that the Bard always had to respond to and preserve.

So there you are, coming back to the beginning. Three things: Stop a minute, wait a minute; establish your direction, find out where you are, where you ought to go. Much more important than how to go there, is the question of where to go, and then the wish to go, the power of the direction. As I've said before, people often forget that our simple wish is the prime source of all our energy.

I think that's all I've really got to say this morning, but I'm very willing to answer any questions that anybody would like to ask arising from what I've already said.

Answer to a question

I understand what you are saying. I think it's a question of how in this modern world, as Alexander teachers, how we can expect to succeed and make our way. I tried to answer that in my talk on Monday night. I think it is so important to approach the whole situation bearing in mind our individuality and the individuality of everybody that we're dealing with, everybody we're in contact with. It is so easy to fall into the trap of forgetting the individual and categorizing people, thinking that because they belong to a certain group they must be *like that*, therefore they must respond *like that*, and so on. No, you've got to observe the individual, and of course our work really depends on individual teaching. It is no better and no worse than what can happen between one teacher and one pupil. If the teacher is successful in working so that the pupil gains the experience and understanding, that is the essence of the whole thing.

We live in an age in which people fall into the great error of believing that you can get vital knowledge from a book or from a lecture or from some other means than from your own personal, individual experience. You cannot possibly understand anything that you haven't actually experienced. That's the thing to bear in mind all the time. You can write an account of *how* we teach, *what* we teach, the *procedures* that we use and so on. But unless the individual reading it has actually had the experience, they cannot possibly understand it! In fact it is certain that they will *misunderstand* it, because they bring - to their interpretation of what they read - their own individual experience. And their experience, like as not, will *not* include the essential experience that we work for in our Alexander lessons, that we work for in ourselves.

I remember so well, years ago, a pupil came, saying he really wanted to have lessons, because he'd been reading Alexander's books for years. He thought he knew them so well that he almost knew them all off by heart. It turned out that he had been a seaman, he was a sailor on one of those large ships that carry cargoes about on the Great Lakes in North America, and very seldom do they run into difficult weather or any serious problems. So that, apart from keeping the ship clean and tidy, and keeping it running on course, the crew don't have a lot to do; they've got lots of time. He had lots of time, and he used that time by studying Alexander's books. He was absolutely fascinated by them, and he could pretty well recite them to you. He asked you a question and you answered, and he said, "But on page 73, Alexander said so-and-so". He knew them absolutely like that. And I needn't tell you, of course, how stiff he was, how rigid he was, how impenetrable he was really to you trying to give him any sort of experience or practical insight. The idea of really freeing and going up was something completely beyond his horizon. He knew from the books what was supposed to happen, and since he knew what was supposed to happen, *he was going to do it,* and he'd been practising it for years! *(laughter)*

Well, that is the sort of problem you will find in so many people. And that is why I am absolutely sure that it's no good looking for some miracle to be achieved by writing the brilliant book, the book that's going to solve it all, that – you know – *does everything that Alexander didn't do, and here it is, highly readable, highly entertaining, absolutely explicit; read the book and there you are, you've learnt how to use yourself!* No. It won't work like that.

So, what have we got to do? Well, we've got to deal with all kinds of organizations and so on. We've got to find out what their rules are. We've got to find out who the people are who made the rules; how *they* interpret the rules, how *they* understand them. We've got a lot to learn, because we are dealing with individuals. And – in my submission – it's the only way ahead.

In other words, I always remember what Professor Raymond Dart said years ago, not quite in this connection, but on similar lines. I think that what was being discussed was the question of proving the validity of the Technique, proving from a scientific point of view that Alexander was right, and so on. And Dart said, "Don't waste your time doing that", he said. "It's been proved, it's all been proved. Get ahead and teach it. Just get ahead and teach it!"

That's what you should do. Yes, you've got to make a living, obviously. We know all too well the economic problems, particularly of young teachers, of people who are just starting and all that sort of thing. But the best advice that one can give is this. First of all, find people, somewhere around. Somewhere in your community there's sure to be someone just to hand, somebody that you know, that you haven't thought of. If you could only just get a hand on them and give *them* a bit of experience, show them something, they would benefit, they would respond; and this is like throwing a pebble into a lake – you start a ripple. And so, yes, they may not be able to pay you, it may seem to be very uneconomic, but if you start in that way, you gain absolutely invaluable experience, experience that you can't get anywhere else. You can't get it on a training course or anything like that, but you can on a one-to-one basis. You've got something to learn. Your learning it will enable you to proceed, and you will become more skilled and more capable. And it will develop from there.

Funeral Service – Walter H.M. Carrington
11th August 2005 – Mortlake Crematorium

An extract from a letter from Walter Carrington to his grand-daughter Victoria Carrington
Reader: Matthew Carrington

I also "want to believe that there might be a part of me that would exist when I am gone"and although I am no theologian I don't see this as a great problem. According to our creed we believe in the resurrection of the body, but I understand that this refers to the glorified body - whatever that means! We certainly change when we die. People say that the soul leaves the body; but does the soul leave the glorified body? I think not! Otherwise eternal life would be a disembodied state and I don't think that is suggested. I don't find it difficult to believe in purgatory because it seems reasonable to suppose that the glorification of our earthly selves will take a little time. (A reconditioning process!)

But all these things are speculative; and who knows? But you and I know what we would like to believe! On the other hand, the integrity of the individual is a matter of practical experience and observation. There can be no question that what we think and what we feel is mirrored in our behaviour and bodily reactions. The whole process of living is "psycho-physical" and we must suspect that this includes many influences of spirit and soul that we are not familiar with.

Ruth Rootberg

Seán Carey: What was the effect of Alexander's death on your group?
Walter Carrington: Well, McDonagh (Alexander's doctor) had given us warning that FM was likely to die at any time, so we were prepared for it, but it was still a shock. Our immediate reaction was to carry on as usual, and we made no alteration in our routine.
Seán Carey: But wasn't there a sense of loss: after all, FM was the pioneer, and as you mentioned earlier, the authority on the Technique?
Walter Carrington: We didn't think about it like that: we simply carried on. It was a question of living in the present.

(*Personally Speaking*, p. 27)

August 8, 2005. I waited for the first class of the Teachers' Refresher Course to begin, greeting a few other people, fully expecting some verbal marking of the moment. John Brown put hands on a participant and began to speak. In those first 10 minutes, he said very inspiring things that brought me right into the work, and then something about "this sad event..." That was it.

During the morning various staff members would say, "It's as if he's upstairs – he could come down at any moment". There was lightness in the room. The work was proceeding. Glynn Macdonald came in after visiting Dilys, asking if anyone minded her giving turns. "When in doubt, work", she said. Ruth Murray, later in the morning, indicated she was struggling a great deal, but that the thing to do was to go on.

The work indeed went on – getting back to basics. Chair, monkey, hands on back of chair – basic, renewing work.

"It's as if nothing had happened," I commented. "Oh, something has happened," John said, "and we will proceed. I think that's what Walter would have wanted."

He reflected that the staff had had two weeks to prepare themselves; how characteristic of Walter's generosity to give them so many days.

And so the course continued – procedure by procedure. Walter's benevolence was still in the room as we worked that week. The staff gave us their hearts and their hands. They worked with quiet assurance, respect, and skill. I felt quieter, more up, more clear, refreshed.

The private funeral was scheduled to take place right after the conclusion of our course. We students decided to have a wake after the final class. We began the last day early, brought our teacups into the teaching room rather than breaking, finished early to accommodate the one o'clock funeral. We said thank you and farewell, and then about half of us stayed on.

People had brought wine, grapes, cheese, crisps. We told stories of Walter. We talked about a question that had been in many people's minds – what it would be like when Walter wasn't there any more.

Now we knew.

In the wake of a leader, the work continues.

Service of Thanksgiving
for the life of Walter Carrington

On 20th September, 2005 Walter's former pupils came from all over the world to pack St John's Church, Notting Hill to capacity.

The service was led by the Revd William Tayor and the Revd Alan Moses.

Peter Roper Curzon played the organ: Bach, Dubois.

The choir of All Saints Margaret Street (Director of Music, Paul Brough) sang some of the music that was in the repertoire when Walter was a member of the choir in the 1920's: Purcell, Vale, Stanford.

Felicity Palmer, accompanied by John Constable (piano) and Anna Beryl (cello) sang music by Gerald Finzi and Carrie Jacobs-Bond.

Richard Carrington read Ecclesiastes 3 : 1-11.

The tributes from Daniel Pevsner, Glynn Macdonald, Christopher Carrington follow here in full.

After the service, nearly 400 people were guests of the Carrington family at a reception at Lansdowne Road. Luckily, the weather was fine, so we could spread into the garden - even so, it was a tight fit!

Daniel Pevsner's tribute

20th September, 2005

It is some thirty-six years ago since I went to Walter to have my first Alexander lesson. What, I assumed, was going to be a casual, temporary association, turned out to be a lifelong friendship. Soon after we met, Walter decided to take up horse-riding again, and that I was to be his instructor. It had been a good few years since he last rode, so, as a good friend, I did my best to dissuade him; after all, he was in his late fifties, injured and handicapped - not good material to work with. Well, as I am sure some of you know, Walter could be an absolute mule when the mood took him. The first year must have been torture, yet he never relented. He had this trick up his sleeve whereby he never acknowledged pain. He did not simply overcome it, in the ordinary sense, he just discarded it.

For ten years or so we kept up with his lessons whenever possible, using various riding-school horses. Then, in '83, when I bought a stable yard, Walter got himself a horse of his own and kept it with me. He did in fact have two; the first, Jake, was trained and prepared for him by my former wife, Gloria. The next one was Badger who in some ways, was trained by Walter himself, to suit his own needs. During the next 20 years, Walter came to ride three times a week, even in the worst of weathers, until alas, it all came to an end a couple of years ago when the place had to be sold and Badger, conveniently perhaps, was due for retirement; he was over 30 by then, a venerable age for a horse.

Walter had all the attributes of a true horseman, and made himself a good rider by surmounting some great physical limitations. Miss Goldie, who came regularly to watch him ride, thought that his was a marvellous example of mind over matter, and that him riding was the best advert for the efficacy of the Technique.

While horse-riding gave Walter much pleasure, it also gave him some further insight into the workings of the Technique. Here, perhaps, it is necessary to explain that Walter practised Classical Horsemanship, which, in olden times, was regarded to be one of the arts. Riding enabled him to follow Alexander's recommendation to apply the Technique to some practical activity, so that one has a better criterion for right and wrong, while being able to monitor progress more accurately. Riding taught Walter not only about his own use but also about the use of the self, in general. From the horses Walter acquired a deeper understanding of the Primary Control. There is nothing like a horse for demonstrating the relationship between head and neck and the rest of the body. A major part of training the riding horse is concerned with the development of this relationship, and the enhancement of it through teaching the animal the horsey equivalent of what we call inhibition. Walter's equestrian research went on for well over thirty years and, by his own admission, had a profound influence on the way he used himself and on the way he taught. Alexander, I think, would have approved.

In appearance and manner Walter was a pre-war, old school Englishman, but his way of thinking, the way he related to people and situations, was a product of the 18th century, the Age of Reason. His favourite philosopher was the Austrian Karl Popper, whose book, *The Logic of Scientific Discovery*, helped explain the process of Alexander's quest and confirmed it to be good science.

Popper's is a philosophy of action and practicality, in defence of choice, of freedom of thought, and against all dogmatic impositions; values that always had a strong appeal for Walter, and guided him, mundanely and spiritually. God, for him, was universal, above denomination. Like Gurdjieff before him, Walter believed that the world will only reach salvation when all individuals attain enlightenment. Although he knew, from his own experience, of the power of religion and of the comfort it gives, he believed, nevertheless, that our fate is in our hands and that humanity is responsible for itself.

Neither Alexander, nor Walter, saw the Technique as therapy, despite the fact that it often has such a beneficial effect on the health of the pupil. They thought of themselves as teachers, not curers or healers. For them the Technique was a method of self-help, which, in order to be successful, has to be learnt by a pupil who is prepared to take responsibility. To Walter, the medical benefit of the Technique was only one element amongst others and not always the main one. He regarded learning the Technique as the best foundation for the learning of skills and for putting them to use. Even more importantly, he thought of the Technique as a wonderful way of introducing people to rational behaviour.

Walter Carrington gave the whole of his being and all of his working life to the cause of the Alexander Technique. He understood its spirit and message, and with the help of his much loved wife and partner, Dilys, gave all his energies to the training of future generations of teachers and to the general promotion of the Technique. Sadly, in recent times he also had to become its protector and its defender. His immediate, urgent legacy to us is best spoken in his own words:

"... these two things – the unity of mind and body, and the attitude towards right and wrong – are the two main features that distinguish our work... It is no good seeing our work like that of anyone else, because it is not. If we are true to our own principles, if we really live the Technique... then there won't be much room for presenting our work as though it was like anything else. To present it as a form of therapy... or to present it as anything other than it is – a psycho-physical process – is to misrepresent and mislead."

Glynn Macdonald's tribute

20th September, 2005

Today we've come together to remember Walter. We have been truly blessed to have known him. Those of us who were taught by him are doubly blessed because he gave us not only the Technique but somewhere from that vast well of himself he gave something special to each of us. From his hands we learned a new way of being. Throughout his life this man, who had an infinite capacity for taking pains, dedicated himself to the Technique that he had learned so thoroughly from Mr Alexander himself. He did not spare himself, he never took short cuts. He saw the work grow and develop worldwide. We have, as his beneficiaries, the honour and the privilege of continuing the work.

In January 2000 we spent the day making a film. In the morning we sat in his study and talked and in the afternoon we moved to the teaching room and he demonstrated teaching the whispered ah. I'd like to share with you something he said:
"I'm coming up to 85, I'll be 85 next May. And I have experienced a great deal of change in myself, and of course, as one gets older, the changes with ageing are very interesting and very significant, because life does take on a very different aspect as you get older. And the great deal of the problem with ageing is that you've got such strongly established habits, which, of course, at an advanced age, are totally inappropriate. You are trying to do things in the way that you used to do them but you can't do them like that. But the more you try to do them that way the more you fail and the more you get into a muddle.

So, it does come back to the same Alexander thing. You've got to stop and you've got to say, "Hang on a minute. Let's see what the situation here is", and "How do I proceed from here?" Instead of telling yourself, "Well, I know how to proceed from here. I've been doing this for x number of years", you've got to say, "No, this is something different". You see, "the readiness is all". When FM gave his books he would write this in the dedication on the front page. That quote is from Shakespeare's Hamlet.

Walter loved Hamlet and he loved the gospel of John, especially John 14:
"Peace I leave with you, my peace I give unto you: not as the world giveth, give I unto you. Let not your heart be troubled neither let it be afraid."

So we remember Walter and thank him.

"Now cracks a noble heart. Good night, sweet prince, and flights of angels sing thee to thy rest!"

Christopher Carrington's tribute
20th September, 2005

Think of Walter, and most people will think of the Alexander Technique. However, for his family there are, perhaps, more complex memories.

The Walter we knew and remember was, like anybody else, shaped by events in his life. He was born on 4 May 1915 just at the time when his father, a Congregational Minister, was about to rejoin the Church of England as a priest. Walter subsequently became a chorister and pupil at the Choir School of All Saints Margaret Street, just off Oxford Street, in London. He then moved on to St Paul's School to complete his education. In his teens he fully intended, on leaving school, to join the Society of Jesus, but was diverted by the Alexander Technique. Shortly before he started his training to become an Alexander teacher, he was still debating whether or not to join the Jesuits immediately, or to wait until he had completed his Alexander Technique training. As we now know, he decided to join FM's second teacher training course, which he completed in 1939.

When war broke out, he had clearly abandoned his Jesuit ambitions, for he married my mother and his lifelong partner, Dilys, and he enlisted in the RAF. It was while on a pathfinder mission, guiding a bomber raid from Italy over what was then part of Hungary that his Halifax aircraft was shot down. His crew, with whom he remained in contact all his life, are quite certain that they owe their lives to his skill and commitment as a pilot.

When their aircraft was hit and on fire, most pilots would have engaged the auto pilot and attempted to leave the aircraft as quickly as possible. Walter did not do this. He remained at the controls to prevent his aircraft from going into a spin while his crew got out safely. He left last and suffered severe injuries including a broken pelvis and collarbone. These injuries resulted in him being kept in hospital instead of a prisoner of war camp. He was released from the hospital, interestingly, with the help of a Jesuit priest, when the Russians captured the area a few months later. After being repatriated to Italy, he wrote that "looking back on it the experience almost seems worthwhile – I have learnt so much about people and things, and above all about myself!"

Walter later returned to flying duties before he was discharged from the RAF in 1946. He always told me that he could have continued flying in the newly formed BOAC, but chose instead to return to Ashley Place and to teaching the Alexander Technique.

These events, and, no doubt, many others, formed the man we all knew and love. He had a wide range of interests, and a detailed knowledge and understanding of a great many subjects. He lived his life enthusiastically and happily in his pursuit of his many interests: furthering the work of F.M. Alexander, riding, reading and music. He supported the Costume Society, the National Trust and English Heritage, the Royal Institution, the Countryside Alliance, the British Field Sports Society, and the Sporting Arts Trust, to name but a few. Although I never knew him to do crossword puzzles, he could always be relied upon to come up with the correct solution when required, because of the great range of his knowledge including the classics, religion, literature and science.

In short, Walter was interested in everything and all subjects. He was wise enough to know that what suited him was not necessarily right for someone else, so he rarely imposed his views on others. Instead, he provided the encouragement and the "means-whereby" for others to take their own decisions and to achieve their own goals.

You will all have your own, individual and personal memories of Walter, but everyone will remember him for his happy laughter, his warm personality, his ready wit, and above all, for his welcoming smile.

Bibliography

Man's Future as an Individual, 1969

A Means of Understanding Man, 1970

Balance as a Function of Intelligence, 1970

F. Matthias Alexander: A Biographical Outline, 1979

The Foundations of Human Well-Being, STAT Books, 1994

Thinking Aloud, Mornum Time Press, 1994

A Time to Remember, 1996

The Act of Living, Mornum Time Press, 1999

Carrington, W.H.M. & Carey, S., Personally Speaking, Mouritz, London, 2001

Carrington, W.H.M. & Carey, S., Explaining the Alexander Technique, Mouritz, London, 2001

Imparando A Dire No (Italian translation of *Thinking Aloud* by Ettore Arcais), Mornum Time Press, 2005

List of contributors

AARONSON Jane (UK)
ACKERS Christine (Australia)
ARCAYA Beret (USA)
ARMSTRONG Joe (USA)
ASTON Peri (UK)
AUSUBEL Pearl (USA)
BARÓN Marta (Spain)
BECKER Yvonne (South Africa)
BRONEC Rose (USA)
CARDONER Jordi (Spain)
CARRINGTON Christopher (UK)
CARRINGTON Victoria (UK)
CHAPMAN Nick (UK)
CHARRON Micheline (Canada)
CLARK Jean (UK)
COHEN Susan (USA)
DAY Jeanne (UK)
DIMON Ted (USA)
DODGEON Brian (UK)
FALCH IRGENS Hege (Norway)
FREDERICK Michael D. (USA)
GEIGER Jill (USA)
GELB Michael J. (USA)
GOODES Dinah (Australia)
GORDON Chyna (UK)
GORMAN David (Canada)
HALLMARK Steven (Sweden)
HARGREAVES Emma (NZ)
HARRINGTON Barbara (UK)
HAUPT Tanja (Spain)
HERINGMAN Jacob (UK)
HOLLAND Mary (Germany)
JACOB Suzanne (Canada)
JACQUES Dominique (USA)

KELLY TANQUAY Kate (UK)
KINGSLEY Noel (UK)
KIRKLEY Donald (Spain)
KREFT Thea (South Africa)
LANDAU Leah (UK)
LANGFORD Elizabeth (Belgium)
LISTER George I. (USA)
LLOYD Gwyneth (South Africa)
MACDONALD Glynn (UK)
MACHOVER Ilana (UK)
MACKIE Vivien (UK)
MARSDEN Frances (USA)
MARTIN Rhuna (UK)
McGOVERN Mary (Denmark)
MILLER Tasha (Canada)
MÖCKLI Robin (Switzerland)
MURDOCK Ron (Netherlands)
MURRAY Alex (USA)
NICHOLLS John (USA)
PAGE Meredith (Australia)
PARKINSON Michael (Austria)
PAYNE Jill (UK)
PEVSNER Daniel (UK)
RICHMOND Phyllis (USA)
ROOTBERG Ruth (USA)
SANDRI Andreas (Austria)
SCHAPERA Neil (USA)
SMART Duncan (UK)
SOLAESA Silvia (Spain)
SOLNICK Sara (UK)
SONTAG Jerry (USA)
STRAAKHOLDER Monika (Germany)
SYPIANSKA Hannah (Poland)
TARMY E.M. (UK)
THOMPSON Ken J. (UK)
THOMPSON Tommy (USA)
VANORMELINGEN Monique (Belgium)
WALSH Nanette (USA)
YOUETT MUIR Judith (USA)